TEMPLE

– AMAZING NEW DISCOVERIES THAT CHANGE EVERYTHING ABOUT THE LOCATION OF SOLOMON'S TEMPLE

ROBERT CORNUKE

TEMPLE

ISBN: 978-1-939779-09-0

Published by

LIFEBRIDGE
BOOKS
P.O. Box 49428
Charlotte, NC 28277

Printed in the United States of America.

Dedication

This book is dedicated to my loving wife Terry, who abides in my heart forever, and to our wonderful friend Bonnie Dawson who has helped with this project beyond what we could ever repay with any earthly measure of gratitude.

Contents

INTRODUCTION

A quarter million miles away, the moon continues its endless voyage of circling the earth. Upon its gray, owlish face there are strange boot impressions left in its powdery dust. No man had ever been to that spot before, and no one may ever return. But if, for some reason, you ever do get a chance to go to the region of the Apennine Mountains, these footprints can be found in the Hadley Plain, about three miles from the Saint George crater. I am sure they will still be there because the man who made them told me that they will last for more than a million years.

I met astronaut Jim Irwin in 1985 at a restaurant in Colorado Springs, Colorado. A mutual friend had brought us together thinking Jim would want to meet me, or maybe it was I that wanted to meet Jim. He was his customarily unpretentious self, without a trace of arrogance that one might expect from a man with a thick catalog of amazing accomplishments.

The one thing that I distinctly remember about that day is Jim describing his lunar adventures to me. He said that he had a new sense of self up there, brought on from a deep feeling that he was experiencing a unique nearness to God. He explained that while standing on the pedestal of infinity, he looked towards earth and slowly raised the visor on his helmet. And there it was, home. It was a warm, living, breathing orb suspended in the cold death of space.

With the thump of his heart beating against his ribs as his only companion and the hissing oxygen seeping into his helmet as the only sound, he stood motionless in overwhelming awe. At that very moment, Jim told me that he knew without any doubt that a divine hand had fashioned it all.

After returning to Earth, Jim felt it was time to leave NASA and head out on a new adventure—seeking evidence of events depicted in the Bible. I was stunned when Jim later asked me to go along with him and search for the remains of Noah's ark on the 17,000-foot Mount Ararat in Eastern Turkey. Jim thought that my police training as well as years as a police investigator might be helpful as a member of the expedition team.

Now, after more than a quarter of a century of biblical explorations, I have been on over fifty international trips, hunting down various lost locations and fragments of history described on the pages of ancient Scripture.

In our modern, yet melancholy, world we want to know precisely where history happened. It is very important for us to be able to stand with expected surety at the exact place where epic events redefined common ground into fabled landscapes. We want the invisible residue of our past to fill our imaginations and maybe even inspire us to do greater deeds as well.

I have stood on battlefields of old as if I could somehow smell lingering smoke from bursting cannon fodder or hear the faint sounds of clashing swords carried to me on the winds of time. But those sounds and smells never came, because the only way to touch our past is from words people left to us about an event or ancient evidence we happen to dig up from the shroud of concealing earth. But even all that is subject to possible agenda-driven error or man's presupposed desired outcomes.

So the final mediator in this book will be the Bible itself. I believe that the Scriptures are the only undistorted standard of historical recordation and any arbitration of facts should be predicated solely on the Bible's final say.

The traditional site of Solomon's and Herod's temples in Jerusalem has millions of visitors each year. They come to the Western Wailing Wall as pilgrims and reverently place open palms and foreheads to the cool limestone blocks as if a warm Divine hand will somehow touch them back. The high stone-blocked walls rising from the *Kidron Valley* with the famed golden dome of the *Mosque of Omar* perched on top, leaves almost no one to even doubt that this is the actual place where Solomon and Herod once erected magnificent worship centers. But, is this *for certain* really the true address of the temples?

There is no place that is considered a more significant as well as a volatile piece of real estate than the Temple Mount. It has been fought over in countless wars for 3,000 years. More blood has been shed over disputes of ownership and control of the traditional temple platform than any other location on earth. But I, and some others, believe the temple was never even there at all, and that the legend of it being at that spot has gone unchallenged for so long now that tradition seems to have sealed reality into a long-forgotten tomb.

Tradition is the remnant of institutionalized customs passed down generationally, becoming forever unalterable. Often the Bible itself cannot even crack open the impenetrable shell of calcified traditions. So attempting to remove the temple location completely off of the Temple Mount will most certainly bring a cerebral dispute and a visceral reflex of heated disapproval.

The Temple Mount is considered to be the most holy site of the Jews for obvious reasons. Muslims however consider it holy as well. Muslims call it the Harm al-Sharif, the place from which Mohammad went to heaven on his horse named Barack.

Even though the Temple Mount is in the middle of Israel it is also solely in the administrative control of Muslims due to some complex political posturing. This is the awkward quandary for the Jews who desperately want to take control, as well as rebuild their temple there. Muslims on-the-other-hand relay a stern warning that if a Jew ever puts a shovel to dirt in that spot, an all-out war may follow.

It may be surprising to some, but in the fourth century, people were trying to find the lost sites of the former temples of Solomon and Herod. They simply did not know where the temple sites were placed. In 70 AD the temple was completely and utterly uprooted by the Romans, thus fulfilling Christ's prophesy that *not one stone* would be standing upon another there.

The temple was eradicated from all recognition, so much so that no one could even tell that the building had ever existed. So, in the next 300 years, with so many Jews having been killed or expelled from the land, people were not sure where the correct location of the temple was. There were at least four other sites that were proposed.

Like so many, I have always thought that the location for the temple of Solomon had been proven, absolutely, without any questions. I, as most all, believed the site to be on the traditional Temple Mount in Jerusalem. But, I began to become doubtful of that traditional view of the temple placement after Dr. Paul Feinberg alerted me to the revolutionary work of the late archaeologist and author, Dr. Ernest L. Martin.

Dr. Martin's pioneering research on the subject of the Temple Mount and the proposed placement of Solomon's and Herod's temples is astounding. This book would not have been possible without his groundbreaking insights. However, I hope that my own personal research presented herein offers a bold new chapter in this potentially history-adjusting subject.

So let the adventure begin as we now take the Bible in one hand and a shovel in the other and dig up some long-lost buried bones of biblical history. Along the way we will walk unknown passageways, known only to the prophets of old, as we search for the true location of the lost temples of Solomon and Herod. We will also lift a candle into the dim recesses of history and try to uncover secrets about the Ark of the Covenant and the gold Mercy Seat's prophetic obligation as it relates to the future Millennial temple.

After all, there is nothing that time and the Bible will not reveal.

– Bob Cornuke

Part I

Temple Lost

CHAPTER 1

UNDERGROUND TREASURE

He seemed to be more comfortable in the darkened maze of the underground world as opposed to being under a cloudless Jerusalem sky...After all, he had lived in dank, dimly lit tunnels and caves much of the last two decades.

When I shook his hands to greet him they were unusually abrasive and vise-like. It was no purposeful display of male dominance; the guy had shoveled uncountable tons of soil and moved mountains of boulders while excavating world renowned archaeological sites. So, it was no wonder that he had a hand grip that constricted around my fingers like a coiling python.

At any given moment, on any given day, with each turn of a shovel, a world-changing discovery might await this rugged Israeli archaeologist. Eli Shukron, however, was not just any archaeologist. He was the Director of Excavations at the City of David in Jerusalem. For more than two decades he had discovered, or supervised, almost all major findings there, including the world famous pool of Siloam where Jesus healed the blind man as described in the book of John.

It was just a few days prior that I had met Eli Shukron. He had offered my research team a behind-the-scenes underground tour of the recent excavations in the City of David.

The City of David can be described as the place where it all began—where I believed that the temple of Solomon and Herod once stood.

When we wound our way through caves, tunnels, and tight passageways, I was truly amazed at the size of the darkened submerged world. There were deep shafts, a myriad of twisting tunnels, and cavernous echo-reverberating caves. There was also a mysterious underground river running its length, a river that the Bible knows well.

While inspecting some of the lower placed ancient Jebusite foundation stones with Eli, the corner of my eye caught the movement of a dim yellow light in the darkened shadows off to my right and above. The luminescing yellow glow was at the end of a short tunnel that slanted sharply upward about forty or so yards. As I stepped over and craned my neck to see what was up there, the silhouetted shadow of a man carrying a sack of which I assumed was dirt passed by the tunnel opening, and then another man moved passed, eclipsing the yellow glow emanating from a dangling light bulb. I couldn't see much of him other than he was wearing a hard hat and had hold of a shovel.

The metal sign dangling on a chain clearly warned that the tunnel was strictly off limits, which made me all the more intrigued. I turned to Eli and pointed up to the tunnel but he seemed to dismiss me altogether and turned to walk down another dark tunnel—and my research team courteously followed. They all were obviously preoccupied, looking about, and were unaware of my interest in the activities of what was going on in the shadowy upper tunnel.

I lingered a few more seconds and all I could hear was the clattering sounds of men busily scratching away at stubborn earth that had not been disturbed, I assumed, for possibly thousands of years. It was as though my gut was telling me to go under the chain barricade and see what those men were digging up. My mind raced with possibilities. I was right in the area where David had crawled up a darkened shaft to capture the Jebusite City, where Solomon had come only yards away to the Gihon Spring to be crowned king, and where ancient prophets of God had walked, maybe right where I was now standing.

I needed to know what was going on up in that mysterious narrow channel of rock. It was as if I was being pulled to that dangling light bulb up above like a moth is lured to a dancing flame. But then I realized that I was a guest of Eli and the echoed shout from one of my trailing team members brought me back to the reality of the moment.

I adjusted my headlamp, looked one last time over my shoulder at the enigmatic shaft and then turned and walked into the dimly lit pathway to catch up with my group. Little did I know it then, but in three days' time Eli would take me to see that secretive shaft and view for myself what was taking place in the off-limits stone enclave. What I would see would change my life forever.

THE DARKENED CAVE

After three days passed, the moment arrived. I met Eli with my research team at the gift shop at *the City of David Jerusalem Walls National Park.* With little expression befitting of the moment for us, he simply said, with an almost sly tilt of the head, "I believe you will want to see what I am about to show you."

"What is it?" I asked hurriedly, unsure at all what to expect.

He replied with measured words, "It is an ancient underground sanctuary dated at the first temple period."

Eli turned without much more explanation than that and walked off, assuming rightly that we would all eagerly follow. We walked behind him in a line down the outside steps on the eastern embankment facing the Kidron Valley. We passed under a canopy of shade trees, and then at the base of the steps, we turned left. We then walked a very short distance out to the darkened maw of a cave plugged into the wall of the cliff. We stepped past a dilapidated rusted fence, barely hanging on its hinges. We inched our way over a precarious narrow ledge dropping off some distance, and then walked over a pile of sand bags stained with russet splattered mud.

Just before Eli took us into the cave, he stopped suddenly and turned. He smiled wide as if he was giving me a special gift that was about to be unwrapped. We had discussed the theory that the temples of Solomon and Herod were not on the traditional temple mount and now he was about to show me some unknown evidence that had been hidden away since the time of King Solomon.

We descended into a darkening cave and the sunlight soon erased into eye-adjusting darkness. There were no tourist pathways, no hand rails, no directional signs or bright lights; it was the raw environment of an archaeological dig.

The place gave off the smell of freshly churned earth that had not breathed air for millennia. We made our way inward, stepping over more white bags gorged with dirt. I knew well that we were somewhere under the City of David, even close to its core.

My heart was uncharacteristically beating faster; my mouth was chalk-dry and a trickle of sweat wound down my back. I'd had this same feeling before. In all my years of exploring the world for lost locations in the Bible, I now had developed an almost sixth sense about these things. Something close, something perhaps only a few feet away was about to change everything I had been working on for so long.

The air became moist, the earth damp and I could hear the increasing sound of men up ahead talking, as well as the clank of metal on metal. I knew from my position that the underground Gihon Spring must be gurgling its stream of clear water feeding Hezekiah's tunnel somewhere in the rock walls nearby. My impatience started to take over, but I could not let it, not now!

After stepping over a crumpled plastic tarp and rock debris, I entered into a limestone carved-out series of flat walled rooms and chambers chiseled out of rock. The entire space had a forest of metal vertical support posts holding up the tons of dirt overhead. Workmen below, and to my left, dug away in a descending lighted shaft that I immediately knew was the same mysterious tunnel that I was so intrigued with only a few days prior.

The workers who were there paid little notice to me as they either hurriedly moved white sacks one by one or ate away at the dirt and rock with their tilling shovels. Eli stepped close to me; it was as if he knew we shared a kindred spirit about these things and also knew that the place and the moment would cause my mind to whirl. It almost did before I even knew what it all meant.

With his Cheshire grin growing even wider, Eli asked, "Do you know where we are?"

I said nothing; what *could* I say? As my eyes, ears, and mind wondrously took it all in, what Eli said in the next few moments turned out to be the most amazing moment for me in over a quarter-century of explorations.

This book is recounting a long journey to get to that place and moment. However, this incredible story cannot be properly told without going back in time and listening closely to what history speaks, and what the Bible has to say about this very controversial, yet compelling subject of reassigning the true location of the temples of Solomon and Herod.

Chapter 2

Walking Streets of Anger

On July 12, 2013, I was walking upon stone pavers in the Arab quarter of Jerusalem made slick from millions of footfalls over the last several hundreds of years. The narrow street, if it can even be called a street, was lined with closely packed shops laden with copper pots, pottery, leather goods, brightly colored linens, and ornate wood-carvings. Swarthy faced men with lips mantled with bushy moustaches sat impassionedly in front of piles of rugs or bins of oriental spices, while others sold from tables spread with heaps of brightly colored candies speckled with nervy flies.

The market resonated with a myriad of sounds and the shouts of *"Hey mister, please come in my shop."*

The clattering sound of an old wooden cart followed close behind me as a small boy pushed a wobbly wheeled contraption that was piled with flat bread higher than he could see over.

I had walked through this part of Jerusalem before and enjoyed the ebb and flow of the daily commerce that I had seen in many other parts of the Mideast. But this time something was very different about it all. This time Muslims started pouring down the streets in old Jerusalem in ever increasing numbers. Estimates from the local police that day spoke of thousands flooding into the soon constricted walkways. They seemed to appear out of nowhere with rapidly swelling numbers and determined faces that were mostly hardened and angled down. They walked in a hurried gait, propelled by what seemed to be an imperative haste. No one smiled back when I offered an obligatory grin or hello while passing them as they came at me from the opposite direction. They just shouldered me aside time after time, till I had to wait for the crowds to eventually pass. I would later find out that they were all heading to the Dome of the Rock or Haram al-Sharif (The Noble Enclosure).

In Jerusalem it was the day of prayer services at the Al-Aqsa Mosque, the first Friday of Ramadan. A video would later show the group Hizb ut-Tahrir reportedly calling for the destruction of other nations. Hizb ut-Tahrir is a pan-Islamic organization and according to the *Clarion Project* translation of the rally, Imam Ismat Al-Hammouri chanted these slogans to the gathered multitudes:

"Allah is Greater! [Allahu Akbar] Let America be destroyed!"
"Allah is Greater! [Allahu Akbar] Let France be destroyed!"
"Allah is Greater! [Allahu Akbar] Let Rome be destroyed!"
"Allah is Greater! [Allahu Akbar] Let Britain be destroyed!"

These angry chants resonated in my mind. It was the same hate-filled tone that I remembered from a long time ago when I was in a jail cell in the Saudi Arabian desert. I was with my friend Larry Williams on an expedition trying to find the real Mount Sinai. In short, we found ourselves sitting in a cell with guards pressing rifles to our heads and threatening to shoot us for being spies—which we obviously weren't.

The guards thought we were Jews and spat on us and screamed in a tone of hate I had never known before. Their eyes reflected the same disgust I saw in the eyes of many Muslims heading to the Al-Aqsa Mosque on the Temple Mount platform that day. It is unfortunate but true, but those chants of hate will be repeated from the mouths of their children and one day may be heard by their children's children (if the Lord tarries in His return). The dissemination of hate will flow like a sewer pipe full of bile going downhill from generation to generation, till eventually they will forget how it ever got started in the first place.

I witnessed two contrasting events involving Muslims and Jews that took place only hours apart, and it all happened in the same general sector of the Temple Mount.

The previous day, Jews were singing with locked arms in the

shadow of the temple wall. They danced and laughed and at times even cried. It was the day of *Tisha B'Av*, a Jewish holiday known as "The Ninth of Av." It was a fasting day for the Jews that commemorates the date marking the destruction of the two temples. This is also said to be the same day that Jews were expelled from England and Spain. Suffice it to say, this was not a good date in Jewish history.

Tisha B'Av is a day when practicing Jews do not eat any food nor drink anything from sunrise to sundown. Hebrews following prescribed edicts would not wash during this time, nor put on any makeup or wear leather shoes because they are symbols of luxury. In synagogues all across Israel, plaintive sobbing can be heard as the book of Lamentations is read aloud. It is a day of pained reflection where people often do not even greet each other at the synagogue because they are in anguish over their temple(s) being destroyed. This display of grief is seared on the hearts of Jews for millennia and it seemed awkward to me that I happened to be in Israel researching the location of the lost temple on this of all days.

Standing below the massive stones of the Western Wailing Wall, I realized that this very place had seen so much war and death. The world has many times held its collective breath over political tensions involving the Western Wailing Wall.

The golden dome of the Mosque of Omar is thought by Muslims to be the third most holy place in Islam. And, as stated above, Jews and Christians believe this 36-acre rectangular high-walled complex to be the site of the former temples of God and the launching pad for Bible prophesy. This place had been taken with force by Muslims in war and retaken by Christians in war. It has been recaptured again and again in so many other battles that many roads leading into Jerusalem today have been pounded out by the throbbing hooves from horses carrying the steady influx of conquering invaders.

To recap all those years of wars would fill many books, but for now, as it relates to the Temple Mount, I would like to start in my own way as to how the feud between Muslims, Jews and Christians all got started.

FIGHTING ANYONE WHO REFUSES

During the Middle ages, much of the Christian and Jewish world had been conquered by Muslims who swept across vast tracts of land like a howling desert sandstorm. The strategy used by the Muslims was *"fighting anybody who stands in the way of spreading Islam or fighting anyone who refuses to enter Islam."*[1]

In Arabic the word *Islam* means *submission* and a Muslim is one who submits to the will of *Allah.* Muhammad proposed a violent strategy of looting caravans and killing many people, but he had a particular disdain of Jews. In 628 AD Muhammad received a revelation that Islam was to be above all other religions, including Judaism and Christianity.[2]

The feud of enmity between three major religious factions had been ignited during that era, but in actuality it had its start much further back in time. In about 2100 BC a man named Abram left his home in Ur of the Chaldees and traveled to Canaan, which is what we know as modern day Israel. God made an arrangement with Abram, and changed his name to Abraham as a sign of his new status. The deal with God was that Abraham's descendants would become a great people who would have the land of Canaan/Israel. Christians, Jews, and Muslims have in various ways made claim that their descendants are rightful heirs to this Divine land given to Abraham. Bloody war after bloody war has been waged trying to settle that dispute of which God had clearly bequeathed so very long ago.

In the seventh and eighth centuries, Muslims had subjugated lands that extended from Spain to India. Their threatening armies made France, Italy, and the eastern Roman Empire quake in fear. Islam ruled the seas with marauding fleets and controlled most commerce, as well as caravan trade with China. Where Muslims conquered, new cities grew out of searing dunes of blowing sand. Many new followers converted willingly to Islam or they were won over by the inspiring persuasion of raised swords over their necks.

Arabs crossed the Pyrenees and held the coast of France, but a subsequent invasion of France was halted near Tours by the Franks (Germans). The bloody conflict was the furthest the Arabs would penetrate into Western Europe, but if Muslim hoards had continued their advancing conquest unabated then the world map would look much different than it does today. A shaky calm followed the Muslim halt into Europe, but peace never lasted long in the Middle Ages with any religion or peoples.

It was just a matter of time till Christians and Muslims would one day meet head-on in a titanic clash of unmitigated vengeance. We know that inevitable bloody conflict as the Crusades. The feud over Jerusalem, as well as the Temple Mount, has been going on ever since.

Some say the Crusades burst into full-blown war when Robert of Rheims sent a written report to Pope Urban II that the city, the holy city of Jerusalem, was occupied by Muslims. Jonathan Phillips, in his book, *Holy Warriors: A Modern History of the Crusades*, describes the Rheim's report to the pope as follows:

> *...A race absolutely alien to God...has invaded the land of the Christians...they have either razed the churches of God to the ground or enslaved them to their own rites.... They cut open the navels of those they choose to torment...drag them around and flog them before killing them as they lay on the ground with all their entrails out.... What can I say of the appalling violation of women? On whom does the task lie of avenging this, if not on you? Take the road to the Holy Sepulcher, rescue that land and rule over it yourselves, for that land, as scripture says, floweth with milk and honey....Take this road for the remission of your sins, assured of the unfading glory of the kingdom of heaven.*

The harsh letter (whether accurate or not) garnered the intended emotional response. The pope would bring together an army to kick the *infidels* from the holy land that had taken the tomb of Christ (Church of the Holy Sepulcher in Jerusalem) from the church. The pope's war, however, needed to be a religious war and framed as a "just cause."

Pope Urban II would make it a very attractive conflict for the high-brow knights of France, who seemed, up until then, to be more interested in fighting amongst themselves with petty squabbles than any far away enemies. He needed to gather forces from near and far to fight those "villains "as they were called. The Turks, the pope described, are "an accursed race, a race utterly alienated from God."

The message from the pope was sent far and wide that killing these peoples would please God and purge Asia Minor of the Muslim "filth."[3] This managed to rouse the citizenry of Europe in strong solidarity as never before, which was a very difficult task considering how insular the populace was.

It would be a grand, holy, and courageous war, or so the combatants were told. It was, for sure, propagandized as a great cause befitting their gallant positions as knights and would galvanize the faithful troops on behalf of a grateful pope and a watchful God. The pope would squeeze every last ounce of bravery from his amalgamating army that were ordered to take back the holy lands from the feared and hated Muslims.

Men by the thousands journeyed from near and far to fight the good fight or die a noble death trying. A good death and avoidance of purgatory is what they wanted in the deal—along with any taken prizes of fortune if they should somehow live. The spoils of war aside, they feared the wrath of God more than dying.

THE "HOLY JOURNEY"

On November 25th, 1095, Pope Urban II summoned the first Crusade from the Council of Clermont. Estimates vary as to the number of responders to the Crusades, but it was vast. Not only the knights and noblemen responded with flags unfurled and wearing shiny armor upon gallant frothy steeds, but the poor came in rags and bare feet. It must have been a unique contrast of social status.

Some were of noble birth with titles of *lord*, who left magnificent stone castles on vast tracts of verdant land. Others lived in daily brutish toil as well as being crammed in small mud-walled homes with low sooty-black rafters and windows covered with a film of dried fish skin. But no matter their station in life, they were all willing to meet death together. They would join as one in a cause larger than life itself, the young and old, women and men, the stout and crippled alike united by the thousands. One witness who saw the gathering army commented, *"It looked like a locust horde covering the ground."*

The pope had plagiarized a similar strategy that Muhammad had used to put fire in the bellies of his troops. Muslims were told that they would obtain favor from Allah and salvation in paradise with many virgins if they were willing to kill or be killed in *jihad.* Per the pope, Christians could also get benefits from God because, according to the pontiff, if they died in their self-described Christian *holy war,* they would gain a glorious entrance into heaven avoiding any refining fires of Purgatory. Never before in history had Christians been offered a reward for violent behavior from the clergy.

Fear in the Middle Ages was also a very effective motivator. Europe was paralyzed by a large assortment of fear-gripping superstitions. For instance, a woman would stand guard over the shrouded dead until burial, afraid a black cat would scamper over the deceased, thus turning the body into a vampire. Ladies of the house would discard water from flower vases for fear that the recently deceased family member would drown in the after-life.

Everything held the potential for evil: demons could live in the dust of the air, in a spider, wandering animals, and even in other *people.* Societies stayed insular and in one place, cloistered together, in the chilling trepidation that if they did not, they would not survive the evils that wandered the dark canopied forest all around them.

Superstitions saturated every aspect of life. If the wind flung open a door, you had to make the sign of the cross because the devil himself had just entered the room. A bolt of lightning streaking out of a rain-gorged cloud would drive whole villages trembling to the altars of the sanctuary. Fear permeated the land, settled in the hearts of all, and filled the church. There was fear of priests, of the confessional, of missing mass, and of the tormenting fires of Purgatory.

The greatest fear of all was that you would somehow provoke a vengeful God and taste the bitterness of His wrath. It was this that drove the Crusaders on to Jerusalem. They knew God's favor would accompany such an effort and if they failed to go or turn back it was an irate God who would greet them on the road of return. So it was fear that lit their way at night and motivated their weary bones to walking in the morning.

With the fear of God, along with the hatred of the Muslims propelling them, about 60,000 soldiers along with pilgrim noncombatants (which included wives and families) headed east in the spring of 1096 AD. An army of 100,000 followed that fall. The scene of their goodbyes witnessed multitudes of women swooning at their husband's departing words. Mothers tenderly kissed their sons' foreheads through hair soaked from falling tears. It was a picture of lament on one side and fervor on the other as the army of the church set out for Jerusalem with banners unfurled into a trailing cloud of dust.

Many Crusaders and ancillary participants died along the way either by disease, starvation, thirst, robbers, or from the many, many battles encountered in transit. By the time they reached Asia Minor, the Crusaders were thinned out considerably by unimaginable hardships. Many noble and proud knights were reduced to riding oxen because their fine horses died on the way or were eaten. Goats, dogs, and sheep awkwardly carried along bundles of supplies. Food ran out, and thistles, vines, and dried animal skins were boiled just to survive. Some even became cannibals and ate the flesh of those they had killed.

A KILLING FIELD

On June 7, 1099, the weary warriors finally reached Jerusalem, but all seemed to have a fresh fire in their stomachs from years of pent-up anticipation. They felt they were being God's instruments on earth, doing His bidding in a final, sacred battle.

The army had left a trail of graves that stretched several thousand miles, but now those who remained swelled with emotional fervency and regained eagerness. They had traveled three long years and had only, until that moment, heard about Jerusalem in words—and now they were actually laying their eyes upon the high walled city. They dropped to their knees and prayed in unrestrained mass hysteria as soldiers wept with reverence and yet seemingly tempered that with pure pent up rage against the nearby enemy.

It must have been the height of insults for the Crusaders to hear the Muslim call to prayer for the first time as it was carried to them on hot winds from over the old city walls. They had all staked their very souls to this cause and it was their moment of truth, their time to fight for God's honor or die in His perfect will while trying.

An Egyptian garrison of skilled defenders waited for them from behind the high and seemingly impenetrable stone walls of Jerusalem. It would be a battle for the ages, a forever hinge in history. And so the Army of the Cross soon encircled the high, stone bastions. Arrows rained down on them, impaling their faces, legs, arms, and shields. The Crusaders were not deterred, and would eventually enter the city from burning siege towers that roared with flames below a sky being filled with angry black smoke.

Warriors poured in with slashing swords marbled with dripping blood. The defenders were outnumbered and soon most were hacked to death. The city was a killing field soaked in human gore. The famous account of that very moment was made by Raymund of Aquiles:

> *"Some of our men (and this was more merciful) cut off the heads of their enemies; others shot them with arrows, so that they fell from the towers; others tortured them longer by casting them into the flames. Piles of heads, hands and feet were to be seen in the streets of the city.*
>
> *It was necessary to pick ones way over the bodies of the men and horses. But these were small matters compared to what happened at the temple of Solomon, a place where religious services are normally chanted. What*

happened there? If I tell the truth it would exceed your powers of belief. So let it suffice to say this much, at least, that in the temple and porch of Solomon, men rode in blood up to their knees and bridal reins. Indeed it was a just and splendid judgment of God that this place should be filled with the blood of the unbelievers since it had suffered so long from their blasphemies."[4]

The few surviving Muslims fled to Al-Aqsa Mosque. The Crusaders, covered in blood-smeared armor, dropped to their knees in a deep display of contrasting pious supplication. Then with clasped hands, their war-weary faces lifted up to heaven as they prayed to God believing that He would be smiling approvingly back at them. The next day, almost every last Muslim prisoner as well as Jews, were slaughtered wholesale. It mattered not if they were male or female, because all were enemies of God. Before the sun would slide into the horizon that day, 40,000 Muslims lay dead. It was a sanctimonious essential to those warriors bearing the logo of a cross that all Muslims be summarily exterminated. But misplaced self-justification aside, it was nothing more than unmitigated barbarous butchery—and the tragedy is that it was all done in the name of God.

The Crusaders were at long last in control of the Holy Land for the next two centuries, and to this day Muslims still seek revenge for that moment in time. They consider the wounds inflicted on them so long ago to have never been forgiven and more incendiary to have never been forgotten. In 1291, however, Muslims exhibited just as much savagery as they had received in Jerusalem. They routed the Christians in the city of Acre, and it was nothing more than vile reciprocity of merciless slaughter. This was considered to be the final major battle of the Crusades, but it was only the beginning of a seemingly interminable feud.

On June 17th of that year, the Muslims broke into the walled city of Acre and took the beleaguered Crusaders by storm. Men surrendered in good faith but were all killed, most by beheadings. Frantic women ran through the burning smoke-filled city screaming and crying hysterically. If pregnant women were found by Muslim soldiers or had a baby at their breast, it mattered nothing and they were summarily killed without hesitation.[5]

During a short offered truce, women were more easily coaxed into coming out from hiding, but if they did, they were rounded up together in one group, and then swiftly killed or were made slaves. The brutal and bloody capture of Jerusalem in 1099, and then the horrific Muslim massacre of Christians at the city of Acre in 1291, bracketed a time period in which opposing religions co-mingled in a bitter concoction of toxic faith. The Crusades were basically finished, but it did little to alleviate the grief and anger from both participants in this ignoble feud. Both sides claimed injustices perpetrated upon each other and both hid behind self-justified reasons for their actions of savage retributions.

For Christians, the early successes in the Crusades gave them the impression that the forces of heaven were with them and that killing was not only noble, but it was to be rewarded by an indebted God. Muslims felt their violent victories over the Christians were viewed by Islam as a manifestation of supreme justice from Allah. And so the cycle of hate continues, and for many it festers in time to a place above any moral balance or the slightest compromising considerations.

The perpetual feud has, in time, involved multiple religious factions. Jews have been hated by divisions of Islam since the time of Mohammad, and sadly they have also been egregiously persecuted by those who call themselves Christians. The Council of Vienna [Roman Catholic Church] in 1311 prohibited all relations between Christians and Jews. Two years later, the Council of Zamora ruled that Jews be held in absolute servitude, and in 1431-33 the Council of Basil reestablished canonical decrees strictly separating Christians and Jews. Pope Eugenius IV (1431-47) proclaimed that Jews could not hold public office, inherit property from Christians, nor build synagogues.[6]

Protestant reformer Martin Luther said of the Jews, that they should have limited rights, their money taken from them, and their synagogues burned. He even went so far as to say that Jews should be given the choice to either convert to Christianity or have their tongues torn out.[7]

The feud has, at times, waned through the ages, and accelerated again at other times. *World War I* saw a huge change to the geopolitical landscape of Palestine and in *World War II* the animosities against Jews were so heinous that neither mind nor soul can ever comprehend how six million Jews were summarily exterminated by the Nazis.

In Adolf Hitler's book *Mein Kampf* he proposed that Aryans are the superior race and all Jews are parasitical enemies of society. He repeatedly asserted in his vitriolic tome that Jews are basically repulsive, unscrupulous monsters that are genetic pollutants. The title *Mein Kampf* means *my struggle.* I find it disturbingly ironic that Islamic Jihad means *struggle* as well. Hitler and radical Islam may share this mutual word *struggle* in their war against all their adversaries, but Jews are specifically paramount in their targeted abhorrence. And so the heated feud goes on and on.

A NEW DAY FOR JEWS—A LOST DAY FOR MUSLIMS

November 29, 1947, was a very tense day because a vote was being taken halfway around the world that would change the landscape of Palestine. The ballots were being cast by the delegates of the General Assembly of the United Nations in Flushing Meadows, New York, that in many minds would set the stage for the fulfillment of an ancient Biblical prophecy. Others, however, saw it as lighting a fuse leading to an enormous powder keg that would end in all-out war. It seems that both sides were correct.

It has been almost two thousand years since the Hebrew nation was crushed and its people scattered throughout the planet like discarded broken pottery fragments. No other nation in history had been totally dislocated from their land and dispersed to the four corners of the world and then come back as a nation unified once again. So it was beyond all odds that the plight of a nation would come down to a single vote.

The city of Jerusalem was swallowed in intense silence that night of the vote back in November, 1947. The only noticeable sounds were the melodic Muslim call to prayer carried on the evening cool breeze from the many slender minarets spiking up from the city.

Across Jerusalem, grey-bearded rabbis rhythmically bowed up and down, immersed in silent prayers. Many Holocaust survivors who had moved to Jerusalem stared silently out of darkened apartment windows with hopeful eyes, pleading to God that the next sunrise would bring a new Jewish state in Palestine. Conversely, Arabs were sickened with the gut-wrenching fear that the next morning would see their land, as they viewed it, stolen from them by the Jews.

Thousands of radios in cafés, hotels, and the homes of Christians, Jews, and Arabs crackled with static as people leaned in closer, straining to hear the news that would change everything. And then the voice of the radio announcer exhaled these words into his microphone. In failed emotional restraint the announcer said, "By a vote of thirty-three in favor, thirteen against and ten abstentions, the United Nations has voted to partition Palestine."

The bellow of a shofar—the ram's horn—lifted over Jerusalem. People began to pour out into the streets. To the Jews, it was as if God's protective hand was once again resting on them. Ben Yeduda Street was soon jammed with people dressed in pajamas and bathrobes shouting *l'chaim* as they opened bottles of cognac and wine. Men were dancing about with locked shoulders in delirious joy.[8]

To the Arabs, however, it was unthinkable; a horribly sad travesty, and unbearable to watch. They had conquered and lost this very city several times over, but this time there was a raw realization in the pit of their sour stomachs that it was all really happening. It was an agonizing thing that would make bitter their loathsome hearts and would add fuel to the perpetual flames of spreading hate.

The Arabs were helpless to do anything to stop the surfacing events that night, but Islam would come to control the prime cut of real estate in Jerusalem, the Harem, where the Mosque of

Omar (also called the Dome of the Rock) has rested since 691 AD. Many Muslims have shown patience in the past when defeated. They had been experts in attacking their enemies after long periods of time and they knew well that time would give them many more opportunities to avenge.

The banners and flags that waved that night are now faded or gone. The wine bottles are empty or shattered just as some hearts are broken that Jerusalem has become a dumping ground of hate. Many Muslims have grown into hostile and vindictive neighbors. Others, however, are willing to live and let live, but radical elements want to kill their way into total control. They seem to want nothing better than for all Jews to be eradicated once and for all. One restraining element is that dominating the skyline of Jerusalem, as well as dominating many headlines, sits the golden Dome of the Rock, still under Islamic control.

Aftermath of the 1967 War

With so many emotions, it was just a matter of time until another war would break out in the region. This happened in June of 1967 and saw Israel surrounded by the Arab nations that made a coordinated and aggressive move of destruction against her. However, Israel was not about to sit back and be clobbered, and proved once again that it could be like a deadly coiled striking snake when threatened. Its air force struck with such ferociousness that much of the air forces of Jordan, Egypt, Iraq, and Syria lay in burning heaps or almost complete ruin in just a matter of days.

There would be epic tank battles and when Jerusalem was taken, the Israeli flag was hoisted atop the Dome of the Rock. All the soldiers and citizens present that day wept and cheered with a release of pure happiness. The Temple Mount was theirs once again at long last. People gathered in larger numbers, prayed, sang, and locked arms in dance. The army's chief rabbi pleaded that General Narkiss blow up the Muslim Dome of the Rock. The general was hesitant and refused, and soon thereafter, defense Minister Moshe Dayan ordered the Israeli flag be taken down altogether.

Dayan's directive has been criticized and his reasoning discussed ever since. But the sad truth of the matter for Jews all around the word is that Muslims retained control, and to this day still have control, of the Temple Mount. It is also a known fact that if any Jew ever tries to take back control of the Temple Mount complex, more than likely, a large death toll will follow.

But the decision was made then and is still enforced today, that the Muslims would be given charge of administrative affairs of the Dome of the Rock and that the Waqf Authority and Israel would handle the security. It can be speculated that if the Muslims were not returned control of the Temple Mount, then a united angry and emboldened Arab world would have come together and a world war may have started.

The clear message is that in no way is any Israeli tampering ever to be allowed in the temple area and, most certainly, no new Jewish temple will ever be built in the foreseeable future. That is, unless there is a miraculous tilt in ideology or a violent act of all-out war transferring controlling interest.

Rabbi Nahman Kahane said that if any effort to rebuild the temple was ever attempted by a Jew, then, "The first nail in the temple would start World War III." But, in spite of such risks to peace, it seems that the Israeli court wants more control of the Temple Mount that will hopefully lead to a new Jewish temple. However, since the Dome of the Rock is so revered by Muslims, Azzam Al-Khatid, director of the Waqf, (the Islamic trust that administers the Temple Mount) also warns Israel of the dire results of any such intrusions.

In a *Washington Post* article by William Booth and Ruth Eglash, December 2, 2013, we read:

> *"...these political leaders, many in Netanyahu's party, want Israel to assert more, not less, control over the West Bank, East Jerusalem and the Old City, including the place known to Jews as the Temple Mount and to Muslims as Haram al-Sharif, or the Noble Sanctuary. 'We're looking for it to be divided between Jews and Muslims,' said Aviad Visoli, chairman of the Temple Mount Organizations,*

which claims 27 groups under its umbrella. 'Today, Jews realize the Western Wall is not enough. They want to go to the real thing.'...'This place belongs to the Muslim people, and no others have the right to pray here,' said Sheik Azzam al-Khatib, director of the Waqf, the Islamic trust that administers the site. Khatib said the mosque is a unifying symbol for the world's 1.2 billion Muslims. 'If they try to take over the mosque, this will be the end of time,' Khatib warned. 'This will create rage and anger not only in the West Bank but all over the Islamic world—and only God knows what will happen....'"

The bottom line is this: Israel is too small and geographically sandwiched between a large populous of hostile Arab neighbors to attempt any such unilateral takeover of the Temple Mount. Also, political allies would look most unfavorably at being drawn into an unwanted war. But that is not to say future emotions will not override such danger-based realities.

CHAPTER 3

THIS SANCTIFIED LAND

The city of Jerusalem has many cultures that are commingled together. The amalgamation of peoples have somehow found a way to daily exist, albeit a shaky cohabitation, while all the while living in the shadow of some kind of heinous terrorist attack. Far worse, in the back of their minds, they live with the ultimate fear that someday a blinding flash of light will mushroom up from the horizon and, in an instant, everyone will all be vaporized in a hell-hot blast of wind.

The old city of Jerusalem oozes with a special kind of history. It is where kings were crowned and just as easily fell in shame. It is where prophets of old warned of doom and wailed in lament when bad things eventually happened. The ancient chiseled blocks there have seen much miraculous glory, as well as hearing of human despair. It is also where the chalky-dry soil drank the dripping blood from a wooden cross two thousand years ago.

The hallowed land of Jerusalem has, for a very long time, been a gravitational pull on many seeking elusive answers concerning their adopted faith. Pilgrims long ago set out to the holy lands from Europe since around 385 to 1099 AD, to be here in the shadow of the Divine. They came in increasing numbers ever since the time that Queen Helena claimed she found the actual cross of Christ, as well as many other holy sites and relics of veneration.

I had come to Jerusalem as a modern-day pilgrim myself. I did not arrive via an arduous journey as had those in the past, but as a modern pilgrimage on a 15-hour flight from Los Angeles. I needed to be in this city, not so much to brush up against the sublime, but rather to find information you will read on these pages.

This book has taken me about 25 years to compile, and as the sailor who is a long time at sea and yearns for the shore, I too want to find a friendly port to dock this work. But I have been cautioned by friends and colleagues alike that what I am about to suggest, as some others before me have, might just create a situation that makes it better for me to remain longer at sea.

Many years ago, I started searching in Egypt for the Exodus route, then continued to Arabia to locate the real Mount Sinai. It was at Mount Sinai that I stood in the searing hot desert and realized that I might be treading on the sacred soil that first held the Tabernacle tent containing the Ark of the Covenant. I then searched in Israel, Egypt, and Ethiopia over twenty-five times, tracing the route of the elusive ark. These many searches are important and relevant to the temple search that will be discussed herein and will be talked about in much more detail later on.

In 50-plus expeditions, I have expended more money, blood, and tears than I care to remember. I have crossed baking desert sands, hacked through tangled jungles, endured barren wastelands, and climbed icy mountain peaks in my quest to find lost biblical locations.

At every turn I have used the skills I was taught as a policeman. After all, examining history for me is just like when I was a Crime Scene Investigator; the only thing different is that much time has elapsed. Every biblical research project I am involved with, I try to track-down historical clues in the same way I did as a cop. To a great extent, history has always been linked to crimes. Without wrongdoing, there would be little in history to record in the first place. Crimes bookmark practically every notable historic occurrence of our past such as murders, acts of violence, rebellions, wars, betrayals, executions and human malfeasance.

Crime, it seems, is the dark, common denominator of almost all major historic recordings. But it is often the hidden and unnoticed elements of our distant past that seem to speak the loudest once they are uncovered. And so it would be on this trip in Israel that I would once again be using my full arsenal of investigative skills from my days on the police force as I attempted to find latent and silent clues that all too often lay just out of reach in the shifting shadows of time.

As mentioned above, in the fourth century people did not even know for sure where the temples were located. Today however, we *think* we know with absolute surety where the temples once stood in their former opulent magnificence. But do we really know for sure?

Over the following 300 years, there were at least four different sites proposed for the temples. It was difficult back then to assign with certainty an exact placement because according to Josephus and also from the words of Christ, those temples were completely and utterly ruined. Every last stone was dug-up leaving a vacant, weedy field, lost to the world.

Josephus wrote that no one would ever know that an edifice had ever been there after the temple's destruction in 70 AD. Yet today it is common for nearly all scholars and theologians to put a pin on the map right atop the Temple Mount of Jerusalem and claim wholeheartedly that this is the place where the lost temples were once located. But, with the deepest respect for their well-intended views, I, as well as some others before me, dissent from this common claim and maintain the temples were located at an altogether different site.

In my personal research on this topic I have come to believe that the greatest archaeological blunder of all time has occurred in Jerusalem, and that this error is the mistaken placement of the temple location on the Temple Mount. It is like looking through a tube for almost two thousand years and then someone suggests that there is a whole horizon that exits beyond the constricted funneled view—that until that point, there has been only a narrow scope of reference.

THE PROPHETIC IMPLICATIONS

It will come as a bewildering concept that the true location of the temple is about a quarter mile due-south from where the traditional Temple Mount is located. And that this *true site* is completely out of any Muslim control.

If this alternative placement is the accurate location, then Jews will have the God-ordained patch of soil upon which to build their so deeply prayed-for temple. As remarkable as it may seem, some acclaimed scholars, most prolifically Dr. Martin (mentioned earlier), have suggested an alternative site away from the Temple Mount for many years now, but very few have ever listened to what they proclaim.

The temple is the key to future prophetic realizations. The tribulation countdown is triggered when the yet-to-be built temple is constructed and the man of sin (the Antichrist) enters the temple and declares himself to be God. Second Thessalonians 2:3-4 reads, "*Let no one deceive you by any means, for that Day will not come unless the falling away comes first and the man of sin is revealed, the son of perdition, who opposes and exalts himself above all that is called God or that is worshiped, so that he sits as God in the temple of God, showing himself that he is God.*"

A great tribulation period will follow, according to Matthew 24:21: *"For then there will be great tribulation, such as has not been since the beginning of the world until this time, no, nor ever shall be."*

Many Muslims, on the other hand, believe that there never was a temple of Solomon under the Dome of the Rock (the traditional Temple Mount). Others claim that David and Solomon are simply literary creations with absolutely no historical basis.[1]

This dismissal of the historical David and Solomon by many Muslims is the core reason that they discourage any archaeological excavation of the Temple Mount today. Arab legend has it that on the Day of Judgment souls will walk a precarious knife edge that spans from the Mount of Olives into the Golden Gate. This gate, however, has been sealed shut since 1187 AD when the Saracens conquered Jerusalem.[2]

But what if the real temple location was in reality, *not* under the Dome of the Rock? What if it is not to be found on the Dome of the Rock/Temple Mount platform at all? What if the absence of

Jews from the land of Israel for such long periods of time, as well as extended Muslim control of that land, has obscured the real site of the temple, which may be somewhere else altogether in Jerusalem?

As crazy as this notion sounds, as mentioned above, there are some top scholars who have suggested just that. And even though such an idea will sound preposterous and inconceivable to certain individuals, I had to check out the possibilities myself. I like the quote from Douglas Adams, who said, "The impossible often has a kind of integrity to it which the merely improbable lacks."

So, to get the answers that I personally needed, I traveled to Jerusalem to conduct what I call an historical autopsy on the true location of the temples of Solomon and Herod. I realized that I would, along the way, need to find the courage to take a big intellectual punch in the nose from a long line of critics who are more accredited and more knowledgeable in this area than I will ever be. But like an old hound dog sniffing at a wind that carries with it an irresistible scent, the investigator in me kicked in when I first heard of an alternative location for the temples.

A "SUPERIORITY" COMPLEX?

The afternoon of my arrival in Jerusalem I checked into my hotel in the old city and decided to take an early evening walk. After winding down narrow streets paved with chiseled stones, I soon caught a glimpse of the majestic Mosque of Omar's dome over some rooftops. It was brilliant burnished gold reflecting in the glow of the summer sun's dying embers. It was known throughout the world as the Dome of the Rock, a most holy shrine of Islam, and just to its south was the Al-Aqsa Mosque. To the Jews the Temple Mount walls are a remnant of the second temple and thus anointed many years back as the holiest site in Judaism.

As I turned the corner and entered the Western Wall Plaza, I could see the enormous stone wall of patina yellow bulwarks framing a high wall of prayer. From a distance, I was surprised at how many people were gathered there. There were thousands upon thousands, some sectioned for male and some for female. As I walked closer, I could hear a youth group of about 100 off to the side singing in Hebrew. The impromptu chorus sounded like pure angelic adoration being carried towards me on the evening's warm breeze.

The Orthodox Jews at the base of the Wailing Wall were not there to sing, they were there to lament the destruction of the temples and to pray in reverent solemnity. It was a sacred district of space and time which was believed by them to be a direct channel to God who dwelt there in a temple that had long ago been destroyed by Romans. I knew there also had to be many Christians in the crowd as well. Perhaps they wanted to be close to the former temple, maybe they wanted to watch the unique Jewish cultural display of evening prayers, or just maybe they wanted to be where the world would see the first domino fall for the end times as prophesied in the Bible.

As I walked down the stone steps, I was soon absorbed by a huge crowd that filled the vast open area, which spread out all the way to the Western Wailing Wall. There were countless people congregating as I maneuvered my way towards the golden dome. It was such an optically overpowering edifice in contrast to the shadowy bastion walls which were subordinate in grandeur.

I knew that somewhere behind me and over my shoulder was the Church of the Holy Sepulcher, Christ's suggested tomb location. It was beautiful and magnificent in its own right. According to the Arab historians, the Muslim shrine was built at its present site so that it would be dominant in posture over the Holy Sepulcher, which was lower in both profile and elevation. In 985 AD Muqaddasi said, *"Is it not evident that Adb al Malik [builder of the Dome of the Rock]* seeing the *greatness of the martyrium of the Holy Sepulcher and its magnificence was moved lest he could dazzle the minds of the Muslims and hence erected above the Rock of the Dome which is now seen there."*

Muslims believe that the site of the Dome of the Rock area is where Muhammad ascended into heaven while journeying from Mecca and then returning back in one night. The rock under the

Dome (Muslims claim) has the hoofmark of Muhammad's horse (Barack), upon which he was traveling on that night journey.[3]

It should be noted that according to Oleg Graybar at the Institute for Advanced Studies at Princeton University, this tradition of Muhammad's night flight was not even conceived until the 12th century, long after the Dome of the Rock was constructed.[4]

So it is recorded that Muslim historians at least suggest that the Dome of the Rock was strategically placed on the traditional Temple Mount because it had superior height over the Church of the Holy Sepulcher. If that is the case, then Muslims did not build there because of any former Jewish temple.

Rosen-Ayalon, a foremost scholar on Muslim buildings on the Haram al Sharif, states that the buildings on the Temple Mount were, "Conceived in a manner and setting meant entirely to overwhelm and overshadow the Christian shrine, (which is the Church of the Holy Sepulcher)."[5]

Today, taken from a Jewish perspective, we have yet another opinion. Gershon Salomon, a former professor of Oriental Studies at Hebrew University says this about the Muslim's intent to build on the traditional Temple Mount platform: "They built those two buildings for political reasons. They used a legend that said that Mohammad was taken in a dream by the angel Gabriel to a mosque called El Aska in Mecca. They changed the legend to state that the mosque was in Jerusalem even though no such mosque had ever existed on the Temple Mount during the time of Mohammad. In this way they wanted to give legitimacy to their imperialistic occupation of Jerusalem and the land of Israel."[6]

In other words, Gershon Solomon believes that Muslims have absolutely no validation in making any historical claim to a holy site existing on the Temple Mount.

THE DANGER OF TOLERANCE

When I eventually made it to the base of the Wailing Wall, I saw many men wearing prayer shawls (*talit*) with leather straps bound around their biceps downward to the hand. A small box was affixed to a strap on the arm, as well as one wrapped around the head, along with another small black box called *phylacteries.*

There were also Jews dressed in the traditional black coat and distinctive black wide-brimmed hats. Others wore drum-like fur hats (a traditional link to their homeland of Poland) with their hair in curled sideburns, twisting downward at their temples. Still others wore Israeli military uniforms with rifles slung around their shoulders as they pressed their foreheads in prayer into the huge stone blocks of the Western Wailing Wall. All who gathered there knew that where they were standing was not only a place of reverence, but a place that is sitting squarely in the cross-hairs of the world's strife.

Most of the people were praying while bobbing to-and-fro in a steady, rhythmic cadence. Some had tears flowing from narrow, pinched eyes; others mumbled long, solemn utterances as they read words from the Torah, but all were lamenting, in one way or another, the loss of a building almost two thousand years ago.

It seemed so odd to me, grieving for what I felt was an archaeological artifact that was long ago destroyed. I deeply respected the fact that they certainly believed that God dwelt there, and understood the profound reverence they were expressing, although I was unsure that this was even the correct place of Solomon's temple.

Hershel Shanks writes, "*We have nothing from Herod's temple itself. True, but the site of the temple itself is not open to archaeological excavation—and never has been.*" The reason the Temple Mount will not be excavated anytime soon, is because it is under the control of Islam at present, and any pick or shovel striking those rocks may be met with angry gunfire.

Jews believe that the Western Wailing Wall is a sanctified zone that allows prayers to be lifted to God via tiny fragments of paper that are reverently pressed into the gaps of the stone blocks. These stones, they feel, are the foundation stones that once supported the temple that held in its holy embrace the golden Ark of the Covenant.

I began to interview men and women who had ended their

prayer time and found that those mature in age said that no amount of evidence could ever be put forth that would sway them from the traditionally accepted viewpoint that this was indeed the Temple Mount location. The younger males in the crowd however (around 16-24 years of age) stressed tolerance. They were open to the opinions of others and they wanted tolerance for their views as well. They seemed to just desire one thing: for everyone to get along. In fact these younger males were *all* looking desperately for the imminent arrival of the Messiah that would unite everyone from around the world by coming to this place in social harmony.

As for the temple being rebuilt, it seemed no concern to them that the Muslims held control of the Dome of the Rock because they believed the Muslim shrine would eventually (sooner than later) be destroyed by God in fire or in an earthquake. It was as simple and uncomplicated as that. No war would be needed. God would do the demolition and Jewish men would do the construction of a new temple and their Messiah would arrive in the midst of it all. Of course everyone would then be tolerant of each other. This word "tolerant," tossed about so freely, ran a shiver up my spine, because I knew that it would be the cornerstone of the acceptance of the Antichrist.

HEROD: MASTER OF DECEIT

Construction on Solomon's temple began in 966 BC and it took seven years to build. It was destroyed by the Babylonians after it stood for some 374 years. It may be said, in other words, that the Babylonians did not demolish the temple, but rather the Jews caused it to be destroyed by egregiously violating God's commands.

Conversely when King Belshazzar of Babylon used the captured temple vessels in pagan feasts, he would as well receive the swift wrath of God when he arrogantly presented the captured temple spoils as a libation to his gods in a boastful display of victory over the Jews. That caused the Babylonians to almost immediately fall to the Persians, who were the ones who finally understood the point God was making. The Persians (more specifically King Cyrus) returned the Jews to their homeland and allowed a temple to be rebuilt, even though it failed to have anything near the grandeur of Solomon's temple.

Independent rule in Judea ended in 63 BC when Roman soldiers conquered the land. When the Roman general Pompey said he was going to enter the temple (which would essentially pollute it with his presence), thousands of Jews fell to the ground in front of him and pleaded that he not do such a thing. But he went into the temple anyway, and was totally surprised when he found nothing but empty darkness.

The temple was in such disrepair by the time Herod took over rule in the land that he started to rebuild a new one in the 18th year of his reign. The temple itself (absent of all auxiliary buildings and such) took less than a year and a half to build according to Josephus. Herod's temple was subsequently destroyed by the occupying Romans in 70 AD after the Jewish revolt. The temples are commonly referred to as the first and second temples, even though other replacement ones were either started or even completed such as *Zerubbabel's* temple. For this book however, I will stay with Solomon for the first temple and Herod for the second as illustrations herein.

It is easy to understand why Solomon built a temple in which to honor God, but for an evil guy like Herod, it is a bit difficult to try and figure out his reason. On one hand he horribly persecuted Jews then on the other builds a temple of worship for the very people he was oppressing. In 40 BC, the Roman senate had chosen Herod, later known as Herod the Great, as the ruler over all Judea. He had served previously in the capacity as governor of Galilee.

As Rome's assigned puppet king, Herod not only needed to keep peace, but he also had an insatiable desire to indulge in his ever-expanding self importance of runaway vanities. Building a magnificent temple for the Jews seems to have been a dual solution that his exceedingly bloated ego cravenly wanted.

Herod was not just two-faced; he had multiple faces and masks of deceit. He was said to be a Jew, a half-Jew, as well as a Gentile. He was a mass murderer, having not only attempted to kill the Christ child (as well as many others under the age of two). He was also successful in killing his wife, her mother, and her two sons along with a long list of various associates, which included three hundred soldiers that he suspected of treachery.

He was so loathed that even his boss, Roman Emperor Augustus, joked that he would *rather be a pig of Herod than be Herod's son.* Towards the end of his life, he had his own bout of comeuppance as he languished in writhing pain and continual discomfort. It is recorded that he fell victim of a horrifying condition of decaying genitals that putrefied and produced worms. His death, it seems, was somewhat of a recompense for the tortuous life that he had so unpleasantly inflicted on others.[7]

Even though Herod built the second temple, Jews today do not seem all that bothered with his resume of infamy. They hold only a lingering beloved reminiscence in memory of the first and second temples in prayers and the phrase, *"If I forget thee, O Jerusalem."* In Jewish marriage ceremonies the bridegroom crushes a glass under his foot, partially as a display of enduring grief for the destruction of the temple. An ancient Hebrew dictum says, "A generation that does not rebuild the temple is judged as if he had destroyed it."

The ancient Jews at the time of the first temple knew that God was with them in a physical and tangible way. The ark was there and the Lord resided between the cherubim and above the mercy seat (at least until 701 BC). With the destruction of Solomon's temple, the Hebrews were subsequently sent away into exile to Babylon. It was as if they once had a firm hand grip with the Almighty all their lives, and somewhere along the journey they had let God's hand slip away—and then they drifted into a lost spiritual wasteland. That pain was perpetuated with the loss of the second temple at the hands of the Romans in 70 AD.

That is why, in Jerusalem today, Jews go the Western Wailing Wall and pray in front of those huge blocks of stone. They believe those hand-chiseled blocks possess an ethereal connection with the same God who once resided there in the all-consuming darkness of the Holy of Holies.

CHAPTER 4

FROM THEORIES TO FACTS

Jesus warned His disciples of the coming destruction of the temple and that not one stone of the temple would be left on top of another. Matthew 24:1-2 says, *"Then Jesus went out and departed from the temple, and His disciples came up to show Him the buildings of the temple. And Jesus said to them, 'Do you not see all these things? Assuredly, I say to you, not one stone shall be left here upon another, that shall not be thrown down.'"*

Christ's words clearly state that the entire temple, each and every stone, will be dug up, dislodged, and tossed away. It is interesting to note that there are massive stone blocks by the thousands in the wall supporting the Temple Mount platform. Was Jesus wrong in His prophesying that not one stone would remain standing?

When I started to tell friends and associates about the new temple site relocation project, they were somewhat ambivalent. They believed that those high surrounding rock walls of the Temple Mount were the same ones that supported the environs of Solomon's temple. That is what they were taught; that is what almost everyone believes. Case closed. That is, until I told them the rest of the story.

When you look carefully at the Bible verse, "not one stone upon another," we find that Jesus was actually gone from the temple when He spoke those words. Jesus was walking away when His disciples came up to Him and called His attention to the temple buildings. The verse continues with Christ asking, *"Do you not see all these things?"*

What Jesus is mentioning is the whole of the temple, being seen from a distance of some unknown calibration, but most assuredly down the road some from the temple complex. It was from this space of separation that Christ says that every stone of the temple would be thrown down. I believe He would have been describing the walls, ancillary buildings, and all.

Historian Flavius Josephus wrote that the entirety of the temple was indeed in total ruin and destruction after 70 AD. He went on to say that if he had not personally been in Jerusalem during the war and witnessed the demolition by Titus of the temple that took place there, he wouldn't have believed it ever existed. In Josephus (*Jewish Wars,* VII, 1.1) it speaks of widespread destruction in all Jerusalem as well. Archaeology and eye-witness evidence suggests that Jerusalem was destroyed so severely that not much of it was left other than an array or meager constructs and some resilient stone towers and walls. However, the foundation walls of what we call today the traditional Temple Mount would not, in all likelihood, be included in the manifest of those destroyed edifices because it was Roman-owned and would be considered separate from Jerusalem in general by Josephus.

The temple, however, according to Scripture, was dug up to the very last stone, making it personal to the Romans. They hated the Jews and wanted this iconic Hebrew building scrubbed clean from the earth. I believe they actually relished shaming and defaming the Jews by eradicating any trace of the temple, and thus ironically fulfilled prophesy spoken by Jesus.

The temple's total destruction, in a small way, resembles Custer's last stand. It was personal vindication of the Sioux warriors that every last man in the Seventh Cavalry was killed on that fateful day at the Little Big Horn battlefield. There is something about total annihilation that makes a chilling statement from the victor—and the Romans would have prized that kind of retribution and achievement.

WHERE IS THE TEMPLE?

Finding or accepting a new location for the precise site of the temple of Solomon is a most difficult task because there is a stumbling force we mentioned earlier, called "tradition." Tradition has hammered a flag so deep into the Temple Mount site (Dome of the Rock), that virtually no amount of historically relevant proof will ever pull it loose from the tenacious grip of man-crafted thinking.

Another pitfall in any investigation is to let the witnesses speak for themselves and not all of us speaking for them. In the case of the famed Jewish historian Flavius Josephus, whom I will quote so liberally in this book, he has been accused of being an exaggerator, and a poor historian concerning his writings as to where the temple is located. Yet, this same historian has been highly praised as being very accurate for most all his other historical accountings. I believe the reason he is criticized concerning the temple location is because he goes against the traditional placement of the Dome of the Rock/Temple Mount.

So, is Josephus wrong, or are we—and have been completely misinformed for over a thousand years? Are we being guided by tradition as opposed to an actual eyewitness (Josephus) who was there at the time of the temple destruction? He saw it, he smelled it, he heard it, and then wrote about it.

I believe Josephus was trying to speak accurately to a future audience with his written history. But Professor George Adam Smith, an esteemed authority on Jerusalem, stated, "The dimensions Josephus gave us are not trustworthy, nor reconcilable with the Haram area."

The Haram area is the existing Temple Mount platform and the dimensions of Josephus, concerning the temple, as Adam Smith says, do not fit in several places because I believe Josephus was speaking of a completely different area than the Haram/ Temple Mount platform. Is it possible that Josephus got it all right and we got it all wrong because we cannot see through a thick layer of cement poured over us from a big wheelbarrow called tradition?

Josephus gives us a vivid description and size of the Roman garrison in first-century Jerusalem. I believe he is detailing the 36-acre Dome of the Rock platform. He describes Jerusalem as being occupied by the mighty Tenth Legion (*Legio X Fretensis*).

The garrison was named Fort Antonia after Mark Anthony, who was a friend of Herod the Great. It was also referred to as the place of the *praetorium* by others in history. The fortress was large, as big as several cities. Josephus used the Greek word *tagma,* to number the amount of men stationed at the fort, which was approximately 6,000 men plus the needed support staff. All told, as many as 10,000 personnel served there.[1]

The Roman fort would need at least the area of the present day Temple Mount (36 acres) to sustain itself. Keep in mind that what we refer to today as the Temple Mount was built like a castle, with walled fortifications and bulwarks for defense, just as other Roman forts have been constructed. Josephus wrote that it was said that the fort was much larger than the temple, but scholars say the temple area is much bigger than the fort. Again, who is right? According to many academics, Josephus exaggerated and is the culprit here. But let's examine the view of scholars who were *not* there and inspect the writings of Josephus, who was.

FROM IMAGINATION TO REALITY

In 1973, famous model maker and historian, Michael Avi-Yonah, made a model of first-century Jerusalem, which is today displayed at the Israeli Museum. His rendering shows the Roman fort as a small appendage to the temple on the northwest corner. His work is remarkable and painstakingly constructed, but unfortunately it may be wrong, and yet scholars seem to not even dare challenge its accuracy. It is hard for me to believe that almost everyone has accepted this model as if it had been chiseled by the Divine hand of God. But it was from the imagination of a man who did his best to reconstruct the past, which is like us trying to sketch a battle scene without knowing *who* was fighting, *where* they were fighting, and for *what* reason they were fighting. And so we have an individual showing a small Roman fort adjacent to the Temple Mount platform to harmonize, it seems, with tradition while ignoring eyewitness accounts at the time.

This has all resulted in us having today almost every television documentary on the subject of the temple showing the Avi-Yonah model as an "accurate in every way" illustrative prop. But it is far too small to fit Josephus' description which requires a mammoth fort the size of several cities. That is why artists' paintings, renderings, and models of the temple today all show a glorious white pillared temple perched on top of a 36-acre Temple Mount platform, and then they awkwardly add a small, almost unnoticeable, Roman fort at the northwest corner.

Author Ernest Martin in his book *The Temples That Jerusalem Forgot,* explains that Josephus wrote of a *tagma,* or legion of approximately 6,000 soldiers, being garrisoned at the Roman Fort Antonia along with a substantial support staff amounting to as many as 10,000 personnel. However, per Dr. Martin, there has been a blatant mistranslation of Josephus' words in Williamson and the Loeb editions by Thackeray. That translation of Josephus is said to use the word cohort in describing the amount of soldiers at the fort—which would make for a much smaller contingent of about 480 or so men.

The big question that begs to be asked here is why did a translator change the correct rendering of *tagma,* which was approximately 6,000 soldiers, and modify it to the incorrect smaller cohort of only approximately 480 soldiers? All of the other times that Josephus uses the terminology of *tagma* in his historical records, he makes reference to a much larger number of soldiers such as the fifth, tenth, twelfth and fifteenth legions. A smaller cohort would certainly harmonize with a small Roman fort as we have in the Avi-Yonah model at the Israeli museum, which, in turn, justifies a much larger temple mount complex. But in reality, this is wrong; it should be just the other way around. We should have a much larger Roman fort based on the correct translation of the word *tagma* which would be overshadowing a subordinate in size temple area. Roman soldiers would never have a smaller area assigned for their fort and allow for a substantially superior in size Jewish worship structure. Josephus makes this point very clear when he noted, *"...the temple was a fortress that guarded the city* (Zion) *as was the tower of Antonia a guard to the temple"* (italics mine).

There is not one shred of evidence that a huge Roman fort has ever been found anywhere in Jerusalem. That leaves us with having to make the fort shrink down in size, as the Avi-Yonah model does, to justify a Dome of the Rock placement for the temples.

A FLAWED THEORY

In the *New Bible Dictionary* (p. 1246) there is a scale overview drawing of the Temple Mount and the Roman fort appendage on the northwest corner. The fort is scaled to be approximately 400 feet by 300 feet. It is absurd to even suggest that a Roman cohort of about 480 or so men with support staff, let alone a full legion and support staff of about 10,000 total personnel, could fit into such a tight area.

Does anyone believe for one minute that the Romans would ever build a small fort right next to a huge high-walled Jewish temple complex? Why would the Romans, who were control perfectionists, allow a Jewish worship center to be constructed that is far mightier in stature and defense bulwarks than their own much smaller fortress? Does anyone think that after building this huge castle-like structure for the Jews with thousands of massive stone blocks (some as large as a big truck), that they would then build a subordinate-sized fort and stick it in the corner like you would a tiny garage next to a sprawling mansion? The concept simply violates all logic.

The Tenth Legion was comprised of almost 10,000 people that included soldiers along with support personnel. It was garrisoned there to keep order in the province and to contain the riot-prone Jews at festival times. During these religious celebrations, it is estimated that 80,000-100,000 worshipers poured into Jerusalem. When you add this to the already 150,000-200,000 population at the time of Christ, there could be almost a quarter of a million people trying to witness the ceremonies at the temple courts.[2]

The flawed proposal that there was only a cohort of approximately 480 men is discounted completely when you read in the Bible where 470 men (200 infantry, 70 cavalry, and 200 spearmen) escorted just one man (the apostle Paul) from Fort

Antonia to Caesarea, as described in the book of Acts.

So, are we to believe that a garrison of only about 480 men would send 470 of them off to Caesarea to protect a single prisoner bound in chains, and then leave the entire garrison practically empty with only a handful of soldiers to defend and control as many as a quarter a million, depending on festival crowds? The idea is beyond unrealistic because they could (and did) easily spare those 470 men because they had thousands more left behind at the fort to manage the hundreds of thousands of often potentially hostile Jews. (See note at the end of this chapter.)

The Romans were in Jerusalem from 63 BC until 289 AD, and all that while they were not scattered about the city, but the majority of that time they would have logically been in a well-protected fort. The conclusion is that the Roman fort had to be huge and, as Josephus wrote, the size of *"several cities."*

The traditional Temple Mount platform/Dome of the Rock complex fits in perfectly with the size needs for the Roman *Legio X Fretensis.* Roman forts were customarily rectangle in shape as is the traditional Temple Mount. Josephus describes the immense facility of the Romans, *"Now as to the Tower of Antonia...it might seem to be composed of several cities....It contained also four other distinct towers at its four corners; wherefore the others were but fifty cubits high; whereas that which lay upon the southeast corner was seventy cubits high."*[3]

Josephus is depicting a huge complex with many thousands of troops and support staff, from medical facilities to prisons, places of worship, food storage, kitchens, stables, horse tenders, bakers, armories, blacksmiths, barbers, court rooms, baths, granaries, brothels, roads, latrines, barracks and officers' quarters. The fort was a sprawling bustling facility, and yet absolutely nothing has ever been found of any structural remains in Jerusalem. Why? Because all we have to do is look up and see the Dome of the Rock and realize that is the location of the lost Roman fort. Then we should look south and downward to the old City of David and say, "That is the area of the lost temple."

In the spring of 66 AD, angry and fed-up Jewish citizenry revolted against harsh Roman rule. It would cost them everything.

Judea rose up in a violent rebellion without any plan, organization, or leadership. But in spite of their disarray, section by section, the Romans lost control of the city of Jerusalem from the frenzied Jews. The streets ran with blood and chaos.

Finally, in 70 AD, Titus came to Jerusalem to totally crush the Jewish revolt that had taken over the city. He arrived with four legions, the Fifth, the Tenth, the Twelfth and the Fifteenth. In the end, a million people would die in the siege and another 97,000 Jews would be taken prisoners by the Roman military.[4]

THE MOUNT IS THE FORT

In his book, *The Archaeology of the Jerusalem Area,* Harold Mare writes that the final collapse of the Holy City came in September, 70 AD, *after* the capture of Fort Antonia. Again are we to believe that the seizing of a small appendage next to the huge occupied Temple Mount would be the tipping point and make the deciding advantage to the war. It was not the capture of the small Fort Antonia of an artist's imagination that turned the tide; it was the real Fort Antonia (which is today the mammoth Temple Mount platform) that was captured that made the balance of battle shift to the Romans advantage and their ultimate victory. In fact the Roman fort in Jerusalem was so big that it took tens of thousands of Jews in the revolt to take the fort from the scant 250 men of the 3rd Gallicia that had not fled.[5] It was because they were not in a lesser-sized fort as historians would have us believe.

Here again, when we look at the fact that there was a massive fort in Jerusalem and try to say we have not uncovered one stone of it, are we so entrenched in tradition that we awkwardly try to cram the notion of a small lost fort into reality? But, if we view the Temple Mount as the real Fort Antonia, a very large and massive fortification, then the gears of history mesh.

So, let's look at the facts in the conquest of Jerusalem from another perspective. Josephus writes that Titus conquered the city and sometime later (before the temple is captured) was found to be in his tent. Runners then came from a distance panting and communicated that the temple was being ransacked by frenzied invaders. The soldiers had not only set fire to the temple but they killed so many Jews that their bodies were piled high upon one another. The noise of the temple pillage was so intense that the soldiers had to use hand signals just to communicate over the loud uproar.[6]

According to Josephus, the destructive actions of the invaders happened while Titus was in his tent—which was obviously in the recaptured Fort Antonia that was held by the revolting Jews. So, if Fort Antonia was contiguous to the Temple Mount (as modern scholars suggest) then Titus would have been within easy ear shot of all that commotion and no runners would be needed to inform him of the ruckus. However, if the fort was approximately a quarter of a mile from the city of David, as I and others suggest, then runners would indeed be needed to convey the news.

Remember these facts as we proceed.

Note:

It should be mentioned that there is some argument as to the exact size of a Roman legion in Jerusalem at the time of the first Jewish revolt. No one knows for sure but in the excellent book by Stephen Dando-Collins, Legions of Rome, which I have referenced, a generally accepted size of a legion and cohort are described as follows: "From 30 BC, Augustus took the 6,000-man republican legion, with its ten cohorts of 600 men and turned it into a unit with nine cohorts of 480 men, and a so called 'double strength' 1st cohort of 800 men charged with the protection of the legion's commander and eagle standard. To this, Augustus added a legion cavalry squadron of 128 men, making a legion, on paper, amount to 5,248 men, including 59 centurions, plus three senior officers, its legate, its broad-stripe tribune and its camp-prefect. Added to this were five thin-stripe tribune officer cadets." So it seems that a general accounting of 6,000 soldiers plus a support staff of 4,000 is within the general parameters as well as estimating the size of a cohort at around 480 or so men.

Chapter 5

A Rock and a Pilgrim

After the Jewish war/revolt there was little remaining in Jerusalem to even suggest that it was once a great city except for some scant damaged constructs, beleaguered walls, and damaged sections of stone towers.[1] It was in a state of pitiful ruin.

So how is it that we still have standing one of the greatest monoliths of ancient architecture that is known world-wide as the Temple Mount/Dome of the Rock platform, and this behemoth of a structure was not even mentioned by Josephus as surviving? The Temple Mount today is so large that it could hold the Rose Bowl in Pasadena, California, and still have 35 percent of remaining space for parking.

Are we to believe that Josephus did not even see that spectacular edifice when describing the postwar landscape of Jerusalem which was almost totally destroyed? Such a conjecture is impossible, of course, because the massive stone block structure was a Roman fort. It was Roman owned, Roman operated, Roman esteemed—and not part of the general city of Jewish-occupied Jerusalem and its ruinous condition. Its existence was obviously and purposefully omitted from the narrative by Josephus who was, after all, recording for Roman posterity.

It should be noted here again that the temple was burned and completely pulled up stone by stone, as Christ predicted. The Fort of Antonia with its mighty walls makes it virtually impossible to be the Temple Mount, if you believe in the veracity of Christ's words.

On my first trip to Jerusalem, I was allowed the very rare opportunity to film inside the Muslim shrine of the Dome of the Rock. I have been contacted by several documentarians from major cable networks who were amazed that I was given permission to do this.

Inside the shrine you stand beneath a huge ornate dome, under which is a large rock protrusion that you can easily recognize as at one time being packed by massive amounts of fill dirt all around its edges. In fact the whole area on the Haram platform was filled in. It would be like having an empty wood-sided sand box and then placing a big rock in the middle of it. You would then pack the box with sand till a small portion of the rock at the top is exposed and the rest would be flat, usable space.

In a very simple way, that is the how the Temple Mount was made. If you examine Alcatraz Island, for instance (which is known as "The Rock"), you have the same thing. There is this huge rock protrusion rising as an island in the San Francisco Bay. To make that uneven rock workable as a prison, with the needed large flat surfaces, you would first have to put high, thick concrete walls around the edges of the rock and fill it all in until it is flat on top. You would then have created a prison that looks like a high-walled fortress, very similar in look and design to the Temple Mount in Jerusalem.

I believe that the Romans did the same thing as was done at Alcatraz. They looked up at this big precipice and knew it would make an excellent place for a high fortress. Romans always preferred a hilltop for their forts and always leveled them off prior to building their network of roads and facilities.[2]

In Jerusalem they first needed to build a massive retaining wall with heavy stones and then fill it all in. If you look at the Western Wailing Wall today you are probably seeing that very same type retaining wall. Josephus says that Fort Antonia was positioned around, as well as over, a large prominent rock protrusion.

A FOURTH CENTURY EYE WITNESS

In 333 AD, the Pilgrim of Bordeaux wrote about this jutting rock as being the pinnacle of the Roman fort (praetorium). The Bordeaux Pilgrim is one of the earliest recorded Christian witnesses to visit the holy land.[3]

The writer gave us an incredible historical gift by describing Jerusalem from the eyes of one walking through the city in the fourth century. The author is unknown to us, but what is written is now eternal. I can't even imagine how very difficult it was for him to travel at that time entirely by road through dangers at every turn and somehow make it all the way from the west coast of France to Israel.

When the Pilgrim of Bordeaux finally arrived at the Church of the Holy Sepulcher in 333 AD (which was still under construction), he wrote some very interesting observations. He said that while looking east from the Church of the Holy Sepulcher, he saw stone walls with foundations going down to the Tyropoean Valley. Keep in mind that the pilgrim was looking due east and was staring directly at the traditional Temple Mount area. He said absolutely nothing about it being the temple site, but rather he describes the stone walls (all of the stone walls) that he was looking at as the praetorium of the Romans. Portions of the wall were still evident. This means that the walls would have survived the Roman/Jewish war of 66-70, because they were property of the fort itself. The praetorium was there, according to the pilgrim, which he said was the place where Jesus was sentenced to death.

So, in effect, if we are to believe the Pilgrim of Bordeaux, the dome over the Dome of the Rock, which is a Muslim shrine, would be the very site where Jesus was sentenced to death by Pontius Pilate. The Bordeaux Pilgrim is very important, because he and the famous Eleazar are the only known two who referred to the surviving walls of the Roman fortress garrison from 70-370 AD. [4]

This pilgrim is the earliest Christian visitor we know of who wrote this all down, but again, Josephus was there at the time of the first century.

In the sixth century the Piacenza Pilgrim wrote of an oblong stone at the *Roman praetorium* as well, and described this rock as the place that Pilate heard the case of Christ.[5]

This rock notation is consistent with the mounting evidence that shows the Dome of the Rock area was the Roman fortress, but most scholars simply won't buy that theory. They know full well, however, that a Roman fort needed a large, dominating, well-fortified campsite located somewhere in Jerusalem and most likely on the high-ground, where most forts are usually situated. The raised position would be advantageously the pinnacle elevation of the Dome of the Rock in this supposition.

In the book *The Histories,* by Tacitus the Roman, we learn that Fort Antonia had a conspicuous height and that it was a castle named by Herod in honor of Mark Anthony.[6]

So how could this huge fort be lost with no one able to say for sure where it was located? It seems that it was there all the while—and is still there today. The Bordeax Pilgram saw it due east of the church of the Holy Sepulcher and we can see it today as well. The Roman Fort Antonia, it seems, is masquerading as the false temple site.

Even though there is mounting evidence that shows the Dome of the Rock area was the Roman fortress, most scholars simply will not embrace a different "paradigm of tradition" thought. They know full well, however, that a Roman fort needed a large dominating well-protected campsite located somewhere in Jerusalem. Most scholars insist that remnants of the fort are to be one day found in the upper city region, but this ghost fort is still missing. The *Palestine Exploration Fund Quarterly* in 1998 stated that absolutely no evidence of a Roman camp ever was found in the upper city. *Bible Archaeological Review* in 1997, in an article by archaeologists Hillel Geva and Hanan Eschel, writes, *"It has been suggested that the Tenth Legion's camp in Jerusalem was confined to the south western part of what is now known as the Old city....the assumption has been that a typical Roman military camp was founded here, protected by a wall enclosing the rectangular plan...This theory cannot be proved. The archaeological evidence simply does not support this..."*

During the Byzantine era, a strange thing occurred in Jerusalem. Pilgrims poured in to see the biblical sites, but almost nothing is said about the temple location. If the temple is mentioned at all, it is usually described only as being in total devastation. To explain away early recordation (of total ruin) by these Byzantine visitors in relation to the temple, archaeologist Meir Ben-Dov said, "It was important to the Byzantines that the

[Temple Mount] remain in ruins as tangible evidence that Jesus' prophecy of the Temple's destruction had been borne out."[7]

In other words, Mier Ben-Dov is saying that Byzantine visitors made no mention of the temple out of patriotic obligation to Christ's words that the temple was in total ruin. I believe, however, that the Byzantines knew full well that the temple was indeed destroyed and that the over ten thousand stones still standing from the Roman fort were just that—the remnants of Fort Antonia of the Tenth Roman Legion.

Another visitor to Jerusalem, the anonymous Brevarius Pilgrim wrote, "There is nothing left there [where Solomon built the temple] apart from a single cave."[8]

The *"nothing left"* notation clearly means no stone walls such as we find at the traditional Temple Mount and the *"single cave"* description harmonizes with geological consistency with the large stone cave that encapsulates the Gihon Spring area in the city of David where a half million tourists a year walk through.

As this project goes forward, I will need to rely on my old police investigation skills as well as much needed inspiration from Psalm 43:3, where it says, *"O send out Your light and Your truth! Let them lead me; let them bring me to your holy hill. And Your tabernacle...."*

Two Sides of a War

The Roman imperial government was nothing to trifle with. If you protested, as the Jews often did, then Rome considered it an act of war.

A young priest in the spring of 66 AD convinced his fellow religious leaders in Jerusalem to stop making temple offerings on behalf of the Roman emperor. The match of revolt was struck. There were other acts that fueled deep hatred and resentment, such as when Herod at one time arrogantly (as well as stupidly) erected an imperial golden eagle over the porch (portico) of the temple. Some boys climbed up and tossed the emblem down, smashing it to pieces. The young students were soon apprehended and Herod had them burned alive.

These brazen acts of defiance by rebellious Jews led to riots and eventually to a full-blown revolt. There was brutal Roman retaliation against all Jews, and within four years (70 AD), Rome would destroy almost everything in Jerusalem as well as commit the wholesale slaughter of most all Jews. It is hard to fathom just how ruthless Rome was back then. They controlled all their provinces with an iron fist and dispersed sheer terror for anyone who dared contest their authority.

In 70 AD, during the war, there was indiscriminate carnage. It did not matter if you were an infant or elderly, no mercy was shown. The thousands of screams of those in Jerusalem echoed down the stone streets all hours of the night and day. Archaeological evidence from Kenyon found along the Tyropoeon Valley torn-up streets included walls razed, houses burned and smashed, and pottery dating to the time of the revolt. The drains in the area were clogged with bones and piles of skulls.[9]

However, there were a few exceptions to being summarily slaughtered, such as being a woman of the right age and look, which made for a good price when sold into slavery. If you were a fit young man, you might be sent to local quarries or slave mines in Egypt for back-breaking labor till the day you died, or were killed. Others captured might be used as props for amusement in entertainment venues sponsored by the imperial Roman authorities—where they were butchered in front of a blood-lusting crowd. Some were even wrapped in raw animal hides and devoured by rabid beasts for the sheer pleasure of the wildly cheering Roman citizenry.

Josephus witnessed the barbaric acts of the revolt first hand and he must have been sickened. When he found someone he happened to know in excruciating agony hanging upon a cross, what did Josephus say to them, and more importantly, what did they possibly say to him? It must have been a gut-wrenching experience seeing them impaled with spikes through wrists and feet, with their limp bodies dangling in unimaginable torment. And, as he walked the streets he would have seen so many other men, women and children lying blue and stiff with mutilated bodies bloating under a cloudless sky.

The writer Josephus was, however, compelled to record what happened, but he needed to use caution in his words or he too would wind up dead from the slash of a Roman soldiers sword, leaving him a forever silent voice. He saw it all and wrote about much as an eyewitness, offering his testimony for future eyes to read and future minds to learn about what had taken place in this horror-laced, episodic era. And like all the Jews around him, he endured the ultimate atrocity in having to watch the magnificent temple of the Lord gutted, looted, and burned in dismaying effigy to nothing more than smoldering ashes. To add insult to injury, each and every stone was irreverently torn-away from the very place that they had once been so dutifully positioned.

Josephus descended from a priestly line and had also been a commander of the Jewish forces in Galilee during the time of the first revolt. At Jotapata, the city fell to the Romans and so 40 of his men fled to a cave. Eventually all committed suicide except for one man, as well as Josephus himself.[10]

Eventually, Josephus would gain favor with Vespasian (the Roman commander) and was released from his heavy chains and made a Roman historian of sorts. He was considered a traitor by many Jews for capitulating to the Romans, but in the very dangerous first century, everyone knew that death was a probable outcome if you weren't shrewd in your alliances.

Josephus was extremely accurate in his accounting of historical events, except for his hyperbolic glorification of Roman officials in battle, which again was a prudent stratagem considering the political nuances of the time. He would, however, come to write the most famous accounts of the destruction of Jerusalem called *The Jewish War*. The *Encyclopedia Judaica* says this about the *Jewish War* writing's, *"Josephus ranks among the leading writers in world history..."* I personally feel that his words are absolutely invaluable in capturing ancient events and completely essential in telling us where the real temple was actually located.

EVIDENCE FROM THE MASADA COMMANDER

One of the dramatic events that Josephus describes in his

work is the plight of the fleeing rebel Jews who went to the fortress in Masada. If you visit this historical site today, most tourists will miss the fact that there is archaeological evidence of eight Roman camps surrounding the rocky plateau of Masada, but no one misses seeing the Roman siege ramp that was used to assault the barricaded Jews in 73 AD.

Masada should be climbed only in the morning. Being that close to the low-lying Dead Sea, the sun rears its flaming face fast as it sends out an unwelcome hot blast. But once you stand on its ramparts, the heat becomes unimportant because the shadow of death forever resides there. Words alone could not adequately memorialize the tragedy that happened at this place.

I could not imagine being up on the protective heights of the fortress of Masada and looking down to the west and seeing slaves and Romans working like swarming ants building that ramp up to the high cliffs. Bucket full after bucket full of dirt was added methodically, and then after a few months the moment came: the Romans pushed up a big siege tower made of wood and breached the walls with swords unsheathed.

They found no enemy and had no battle: 960 Jews had committed suicide. Two frightened women and five trembling children were all that were left hiding in a rock-hewn cistern. The soldiers walked among the dead, stunned. There was no victory for them that day. They found rows of corpses with throats slit. I could just disturbingly imagine children holding their mother's hand as fathers did the unfathomable deed. Then the mothers held their husbands hands as he slit their throats respectively. Lots were drawn for those who would kill the remaining souls.

The usually hardened Roman soldiers were uncharacteristically unsettled at the surreal scene of systematic suicide all around them.[11]

One stilled voice from Masada still speaks to us today. He was a very important eyewitness to events described in this book, and offers a huge piece of evidence on the temple location. His name is Eleazar Bin Jari—commander of the Jewish rebels at Masada.

It was he, in 73 AD, who encouraged so many in that high

mountain fortress that suicide was the answer rather than surrendering to General Silva and the Romans. He was the one who said it was far better to die than to become slaves to the Romans.

This same Eleazar memorialized the following about the destruction in Jerusalem: "It [Jerusalem] is now demolished to the very foundations, and hath nothing left but that monument of it preserved, I mean the camp of those [the Romans] that hath destroyed it, which still dwells upon its ruins."[12]

Eleazar is documenting that Jerusalem was eradicated with nothing standing, except the Roman camp called the Antonia Garrison Fort with its high stone walls still standing. This can only mean that (according to Eleazar) the Temple Mount (Roman fort) survived, in part, because it was a camp of the *Tenth Legion of Rome.* On the other hand, Eleazer clearly says that the temple was gone completely, even its very foundations were uprooted, thus fulfilling the prophesy of our Lord.

It can be surmised that years later, when the Roman fort was mostly still standing and subsequent conquerors came to the place of those high stone block walls, they must have believed that the magnificent fortress had to be something of major importance. To some, it was the site of Solomon's temple. It eventually became adopted as very special real estate for three major faiths. A new temple home was instituted and chiseled forever in the stone face of history as well as the huge stone blocks of the formerly known fort called Antonia.

THE TWO BRIDGES

On the worn, frayed pages of the past, there is a small clue that often goes unnoticed. It seems that Josephus wrote that the distance between the temple and the Roman fort was exactly one *stade* (approximately 600 feet). Josephus recorded that King Herod built two side-by-side bridges (*Jewish Wars,* VI.2,6, and II.15,6) connecting the gap between the temple and the Roman fort (refer to Cornfeld translation as well as *The Temples That Jerusalem Forgot,* p.413).

The fort was there to protect the temple by the Romans and also allow them to keep a watch over the often insubordinate and rebellious Jews. These two side-by-side colonnades must have looked like two modern raised narrow freeways (or as "limbs" as Josephus describes them) that spanned the 600-foot gap between the temple and fort.

In 70 AD, when the Roman general, Titus, destroyed the temple, Josephus described a battle on these two colonnaded bridges. With slashing swords and hissing arrows, the advancing Roman soldiers tried to force their way into the blocked temple complex. The struggle that ensued ebbed and flowed with one side pushing forward, and then back, and then forward again. The colonnade bridges were about 45 feet wide with a roof that allowed the soldiers to carry their bulky shields, long spears, and swords.

Most scholars do not mention these two colonnade/bridges at all because they do not fit into the traditional Temple Mount location scenarios. Some, it seems, will say that Josephus is wrong in his account of these two bridges and that he just made them up. Contrarians to the Josephus narrative want the temple to be situated on the Temple Mount as it has been assumed for a very long time. But it is hard to ignore Josephus who said, "Now as to the tower of Antonia, it was situated at the corner of the two cloisters [colonnades] of the court of the temple, of that on the west, and that on the north." [13]

According to Ernest Martin, Fort Antonia was located on the north side of the temple (City of David location). If, in fact, the temple was positioned in the old City of David then it would fit perfectly with the two colonnades' separation that Josephus describes as linking Fort Antonia at its southwest angle. That would put the whole of the temple's northern wall as being parallel to the southern wall of Fort Antonia with a gap of approximately 600 feet distance (north to south) between the two.[14]

This would make the center of the temple building roughly a thousand feet or so south of the Dome of the Rock/traditional Temple Mount complex on the southeast ridge in the Opel mound area abutting the Kidron Valley.

When the temple itself was burnt to the ground during the war of 70 AD, its lofty foundation stones were said to be dug up completely by the soldiers. One reason the temple was so utterly and completely ravaged was the fact that the soldiers set out to retrieve the melted gold that seeped between and below the gaps in the stones' joints. Again, this helped fulfill Christ's prophecy that," *Not one stone would remain upon another.*"

After the fire, piles of burnt corpses were found at the altar of the temple that had accumulated so high they slid all the way down to the steps of the sanctuary.[15]

It must have been a horrible sight to see Roman soldiers destroying the temple with such vile intentions, and also witnessing faithful Jews running head-long into the consuming flames without pause in a futile attempt to save their cherished temple.

Today, Jews face strict opposition by the Muslims to rebuild the temple on their sacred place of the Dome of the Rock. But what if Jews were free to build their temple at another location? A place that the Bible and history seems to be crying out, "I am the heir of David, the location of the threshing floor, the place of God, My holy mountain, the place of Zion which is ordained by the Almighty to possess the rightful inheritance as to where the Lord will dwell in His temple forever and all nations will be gathered unto it."

CHAPTER 6

CITY OF DAVID

If there was ever an "X marks the spot" location for the temple, it is the City of David. The Bible says it is there, history records it is there, and God designated it to be there.

Three thousand years ago, the City of David was about 12 acres in size and had an estimated population of only around 2,000 people.[1]

It is a finger of land just south of the present traditional Temple Mount. As a former policeman, I would like at this point to lay out a linear case for the City of David as the one and only place for the temple, but first a brief history.

The Jebusite fortification was a fortress, albeit a small one, but it had what David wanted. It was strategically situated, had a high walled castle-looking complex rising majestically from the Kidron Valley. A spring flowed abundantly inside with clear pure water which made it even more desirable.

The Bible tells us that while David and his army were outside looking up at the Jebusite stronghold, there, standing defiant on the top of the walls were men hollering down mockingly. Second Samuel 5:6-10 describes it this way:

> *"You shall not come in here; but the blind and the lame will repel you," thinking, "David cannot come in here." Nevertheless David took the stronghold of Zion (that is, the City of David). Now David said on that day, "Whoever climbs up by way of the water shaft and defeats the Jebusites (the lame and the blind, who are hated by David's soul), he shall be chief and captain." Therefore they say, "The blind and the lame shall not come into the*

house." Then David dwelt in the stronghold, and called it the City of David. And David built all around from the Millo and inward. So David went on and became great, and the Lord God of hosts was with him."

David took control of what the Bible calls the *Stronghold of Zion* (*Metsudat Tsion*), that is, the *City of David.* These last two locales (Stronghold of Zion and the City of David) are the *huge keys* to solving the riddle as to where the true temple is located.

But to keep on a straight path regarding the true temple site, let's go back to David capturing the City of David from the Jebusites. After he was in his newly taken fortress, David was visited by an angel of the Lord that pointed out the desired patch of real estate within the city walls that David was to purchase from Araunah (Ornan) the Jebusite (2 Samuel 24:18-25).

This land purchase was for a threshing floor—usually comprised of a level area paved with flat stones where grain is tossed in the air and the wind carries away the lighter chaff (worthless husks of broken straw) and leaves the heavier kernel of wheat to fall on the threshing floor.

It is interesting that David had captured the 12-acre fortress by force, yet God was now ordering David to pay money to the Jebusite owner for a threshing floor. But this comment in Scripture is a huge clue for the temple location. In 2 Chronicles 3:1 we read: *"Now Solomon began to build the temple at the house of the Lord at Jerusalem...at the place that David had prepared on the threshing floor of Ornan the Jebusite."*

This verse conclusively says that the temple will be built in the strict boundary of the City of David at the place of the threshing floor bought from the Jebusite. This should settle the matter of where Solomon built his temple. But, because of the traditions of the temple being situated north of there on the Temple Mount/Dome of the Rock platform, it is difficult to change people's adopted understandings—even with the Bible saying otherwise. So to get more answers, let's stay on our linear path and continue on.

A CITY LOST

Over time, the temple was built by Solomon, but it was destroyed by the Babylonians in 586 BC, only to have other successive temples rebuilt in far less grandeur, then finally ending with Herod building his temple where Christ actually visited on many occasions. Herod's temple was destroyed, just as Jesus predicted, down to the very last stone.

Author Ahron Horovitz says, *"The City of David was so completely forgotten that during the Byzantine Period even Jerusalem's biblical name "Zion"' shifted to the southern portion of the "Western Hill" which is called Mount Zion to this day. The Byzantine "Church of Holy Zion" (Hagia Zion), built in 390 C.E. reinforced the mistake."*

Since the temple was reduced to rubble in 70 AD, the City of David was then lost to weeds and abandonment. As time passed, no one knew where it really was. And since the Stronghold of Zion was in the City of David, Zion had vanished as well.

The City of David was gone; its walls were no more—and the huge clue for the temple being located by the threshing floor was erased from history as well. And when something has vanished that held such huge importance, people will stick a flag of indelible proclamation in the ground and make said declaration purely out of need.

That is what happened to Zion. It was lost, so this moniker of a nation, this cherished parcel of land had to be someplace—so, historians erroneously moved Zion without any substantiated reason to another spot in Jerusalem. When you go to the Holy City today, road signs will point to the upper city and the signs read "Zion," with an arrow pointing away from the real, original location of Zion in the City of David.

For almost two millennia, Zion and the City of David laid silently together, buried in a forgotten tomb of earth. Its pummeled ruins were so completely burned and decimated that over the years even its contours were drastically cut down, making it unrecognizable.

The southern part was made into a quarry by Hadrian, who

wanted this city so mangled that it would be forever dismissed from memory. Just think of it, this nexus of the kingdom of Israel, this mighty high-walled fortress of the City of David, the stronghold of Zion, had been reduced to a barren and gouged-out finger of forgotten land.

AN UNDERGROUND SPRING

In time, it would be a windswept field known only to the farmer's plow or a place to dump trash. Zion was forgotten, that is, until explorers came to Jerusalem with a pick in one hand and a Bible in the other. These explorers found the forgotten city with its ancient gurgling Gihon Spring. This hidden subterranean world would cry out that the City of David has been found and Zion was once more known.

Charles Warren, in the latter part of the 1800s, was one of those early explorers. He entered these stone encapsulated environs with coils of rope, ladder, lifted lantern and an intrepid heart. He wanted at first to dig under the Muslim-controlled Temple Mount area, but the Muslims refused his *firman* (license) to dig. So he decided to start in the area of the springs of Gihon and then tunnel under the ground towards the Temple Mount. In the subterranean darkness, he found ancient fortifications, which he called the Ophel Wall. He eventually discovered a wide shaft descending down, which we know today as Warren's Shaft. It dated to the time of David.[2] He knew the water was coming from somewhere, but could not find the originating source.

Warren wanted to locate the source of the Gihon Spring, but never did, and no one ever has. But what he did find was an impressive large underground shaft going straight up at the Gihon Spring area that, if the temple were somewhere above, would offer access to a vast supply of water.

Another amazing discovery around that time (1880) involved a couple of adventurous boys who were poking about in a tunnel filled with water and came upon an inscription dating from the eighth century BC. It was an inscription that identified what is referred to today as Hezekiah's Tunnel. This "water tunnel find" made it unquestioned as being the Zion location within the confines of the City of David. The following biblical verse makes that point with unalterable clarity: *"This same Hezekiah also stopped the water outlet of Upper Gihon, and brought the water by tunnel to the west side of the City of David"* (2 Chronicles 32:30).

The lost city had been found and thus the lost and misplaced Zion had been accurately located as well. So one would think that if the Bible says that the temple was built in the City of David, the world would rejoice and embrace the fact, but let me emphasize again—tradition is a massive anchor that is hard to dislodge once it is embedded in time.

That discovery in 1880 almost single-handedly blasted to pieces the false understanding of Zion's placement on the upper city hill area. Hezekiah's Tunnel was found (even though there is argument as to what extent Hezikiah's workers had in the actual chiseling away of certain sections of the City of David). So one might assume that Zion itself should have been reassigned to its proper place in the City of David location—but incredulously, it was not.

One might easily surmise that Zion was not moved to its true placement because that would completely overturn the apple cart of staid tradition that the temple was on the Temple Mount. It seems that virtually no one wanted the temple location changed to its correct placement, nor was it even questioned in spite of revealing discoveries that had been made. So Zion (the real and true temple location) was not relocated to its proper and rightful site in the City of David.

THE INTERSECTION

To illustrate that Zion, the City of David, and the temple all intersect as one, I offer the following synopsis:

2 Samuel 5:7	Zion=City of David
Joel 2:1	Zion=My holy mountain=temple
Joel 3:17	Zion=My holy mountain=temple

Joel 3:21	Zion= where the Lord dwells=temple
Psalm 2:6	Zion=My holy hill=Christ reigning =temple
Psalm 9:11	Zion=where the Lord dwells=temple
Psalm 20:2	Zion=from sanctuary=from temple
Psalm 65:1,4	Zion=Your holy temple
Psalm 102:16,19	Zion=sanctuary=City of David=temple
Psalm 132:8,13	Zion=ark resting place=City of David= temple
Isaiah 2:3	Zion=Mountain of the Lord=House of the God of Jacob=temple
Isaiah 24:23	Zion=Lord of hosts reigning=place of temple
Isaiah 66:20	Zion=My holy Mountain=house of the Lord=temple
2 Chronicles 3:1	Zion=Jebusite city=City of David=temple

Over years past, archaeological experts such as Macalister, Duncan, Kenyon, and Shiloh, have dug away at the thick perimeter walls of the City of David. The stone walls unearthed there are today a defining template that clearly outlines the tract of land that is the rightful heir to the Lord's House.

Zion (as stated before) has proven to be one of the most confusing geographical designations in all history. It is bewildering because Zion, as a physical site, has wandered all over the map many times. Since the City of David was lost to historians long ago, Zion moved to other locations out of pure necessity. To find the truth, however, we need to let the evidence be the historical vector.

CONJECTURE? OR CERTAINTY?

Robert Ballard, who discovered the resting place of the *Titanic*, looked in the Atlantic for the correct spot where the vessel sank. If he searched in the Pacific, he still would be looking in vain. So if we are ever going to find the temple location, we need to begin where it was originally moored. That can only be squarely in the

City of David, which was the place of the stronghold of Zion (2 Samuel 5:7).

When the City of David was missing to scholars and worshipers (long before it was rediscovered in the late 1800s), people in the middle ages looked to the most attractive feature in Jerusalem as a potential candidate site for their lost temple. The scant few Jews living in Jerusalem then, along with the influx of Christian pilgrims and crusaders, began suggesting that the impressive high-walled fortress of the Dome of the Rock was the actual foundation stones of Solomon's temple. After all, it was the most impressive structure that was still standing in Jerusalem, so some assumed it must have certain historical prominence—and that prominence was considered to be the temple itself.

The idea of the Temple Mount (traditional site that we have today) was not unanimously accepted as the final designation of the temple placement until around 1169. It was then that Benjamin Tudela proclaimed emphatically that Muslim Haram al-Sharif, The Roman Fort Antonia, and the traditional Temple Mount platform was to be forevermore the proper placement of Solomon's temple.[3]

Tudela made this pronouncement with such surety and vigor that it was dogmatically adopted and is fervently accepted as uncontested fact to this day. But tradition has annoying enemies called time, the Bible, credible eyewitnesses, and people with shovels.

If there ever was a most esteemed and believable eyewitness outside the Bible as to the true temple location, it is Eusebius, the third and fourth century curator of the Library at Caesarea. He was a renowned scholar both then and today. He wrote, *"The hill called Zion and Jerusalem, the building there, that is to say, the temple, the Holy of Holies, the Altar, and whatever else was there dedicated to the glory of God have been utterly removed or shaken, in fulfillment of the word."*[4]

So here we have the prominent Eusebius clarifying with narrow and crystal certainty where the temple was located. He tells us that Zion is the temple site as mentioned in his writings and further notes only a few lines later that sadly, after the ruin of Zion

(City of David), the very stones from *"the temple itself and from its ancient sanctuary* were scavenged from the temple site in Zion and used for the construction of *"idol temples and of theatres for the populous."*

If I take the words of Eusebius and assemble them into a paraphrased short paragraph it would read as follows: *Zion is the place of the temple, the Holy of Holies as well as the Altar. Everything there was shaken down and subsequently ruined. The scattered stones from the ancient destroyed sanctuary (in Zion/City of David) were all carried away and made into secular structures demeaning to God.*

And so Zion continually pings the bright dot that appears on the radar screen of history for the exact coordinates of the temple location, but it seems no matter how bright a light this might signal, it does not seem to concern those who wear comfortable tradition over the uncomfortable reality of truth.

We find another credible eyewitness during the time of Alexander the Great, known as Hecateus of Abdera. He testified that the temple was not only in Zion, but located "nearly in the very center of the City of David."[5] And since we have ancient Hebrew writings attesting to this location, this would discount the temple on the Dome of the Rock.

Perhaps this book has spurred a multitude of emotions. Some will be curious to go forward, and others may be provoked to resentment. However, the true arbitrator is found in the pages of the Bible.

For this reason, in the next chapter, I will present the verses that link together the City of David with Zion, the temple, and the Gihon Spring. These are essential to unearthing the true temple placement.

CHAPTER 7

WHAT DOES THE BIBLE SAY?

In my opinion, Dr. Chuck Missler is one of the smartest people on the planet. The esteemed author often hosts conferences that debate prophetic events and biblical truths with world-renowned archaeologists and scholars. His imposing stature and white-grey hair make him stand out in any crowd, but those who have studied his work know that he possesses a mind that seems as if it were powered with atomic energy.

I happened to run into Dr. Chuck at a prophesy conference in Colorado Springs, Colorado, where he and I were lecturing in the summer of 2013. In the past, Chuck and I had been involved in research on the Ark of the Covenant in Ethiopia. He lectures all over the world and those who hear him, even though some can't keep up with his dizzying intellect, love his lessons on all aspects of the Bible. And so it was a nervous moment for me to tell Chuck about the Temple Mount theory. He had not heard such reasoning in all his many years of dialoging with some of the world's best minds on the subject.

"Off the Temple Mount and in the City of David?" he asked with his trademark resolute stare. I nodded tenuously, and went on, thinking I was about to be crawling into an intellectual wood chipper. He sat down in the hotel lobby where we were staying and said, "My old bones need a rest, but you certainly have my curiosity."

I explained to Chuck that the Bible relates how the temple and Zion all laminate over the City of David. I expressed that it does not matter how much mental gymnastics scholars throw at this subject, if they rely on the veracity of Scripture, the temple has to be in the former confines of the City of David—which in no way is on the traditional Temple Mount platform. I told him that as a police investigator, I learned to use a system called *logic connectors*. If one thing is foundational and linked to another string of reliable connections and they are then seamed together, it should make for a reasoned and factual conclusion. I laid out all the following:

- 2 Samuel 5:7: ***"Nevertheless, David took the stronghold of Zion (that is, the City of David)."*** Zion is undoubtedly within the City of David.
- Joel 3:17: ***"So shall you know that I am the Lord your God, dwelling in Zion My holy mountain."*** "My holy Mountain," (temple) is, without question, in Zion within the City of David.
- Joel 2:1: ***"Blow the trumpet in Zion, and sound an alarm in My holy mountain!"*** "My holy mountain" is the temple in Zion.
- Psalm 132:8,13: ***"Arise, O Lord, to Your resting place, You and the ark of Your strength...For the Lord has chosen Zion; He has desired it for His dwelling place."*** The "ark of Your strength" is the Ark of the Covenant. The temple will house the ark in prophecy and Zion is God's chosen place for that, as well as the temple placement.
- Psalm 2:6: ***"Yet I have set My King on My holy hill of Zion."*** The word *King* is for Christ in this verse, and *holy hill* is the temple location in Zion.
- Psalm 102:16,19: ***"For the Lord shall build up Zion...For He looked down from the height of His sanctuary; from heaven the Lord viewed the earth."*** Zion and sanctuary/temple are the same location.
- Isaiah 2:3: ***"Come let us go up to the mountain of the Lord. To the house of the God of Jacob...For out of Zion shall go forth the law..."*** Mountain of the Lord," is the temple at Zion.

- Isaiah 24:23: *"For the Lord of hosts will reign on Mount Zion..."* This is Christ reigning in the temple at Zion.
- Psalm 20:2: *"May He send you help from the sanctuary and strengthen you out of Zion."* Sanctuary is the temple at Zion.
- Psalm 9:11: *"Sing praises to the Lord, who dwells in Zion!"* The Lord dwells in the temple at Zion.
- Joel 3:21 *"For the Lord dwells in Zion."* He resides in the temple at Zion.
- Psalm 65:1,4: *"Praise is awaiting you, O God, in Zion... We shall be satisfied with the goodness of Your house, of Your holy temple."* The holy temple is at Zion.
- Isaiah 66:20, *"'...to My holy mountain Jerusalem,' says the Lord, 'as the children of Israel bring an offering in a clean vessel into the house of the Lord.'"* "My holy mountain" is connected to "the house of the Lord's temple" (see Joel 3:17 above). The temple is self-evident as being in Zion.
- 2 Chronicles 3:1: *"Now Solomon began to build the house of the Lord at Jerusalem...at the place that David had prepared on the threshing floor of Ornan the Jebusite."* This verse conclusively says that the temple will be built in the strict boundary of the City of David which was the same boundary of the Jebusite city.

THE CONVERGENCE OF SCRIPTURE

I reiterated to Dr. Missler that Zion is the place which links everything together. It is the flaming arrow of all clues that flies directly at the heart of the City of David and the true temple location. No matter how hard scholars may try to divorce the two places, they cannot. The stronghold of Zion (*Metsudat Tsion*) is in the narrow limits of the 12-acre parcel of land known as the City of David. If we find Zion we are at the true temple location—since they are forever linked as one in eternity. These three destinations cannot be severed by the meat cleaver of tradition no matter how strong, long standing, or entrenched those traditions may be. So if we use the Bible as the mediator, there is no other place the temples can be positioned but within the confines of the stronghold of Zion.

Chuck leaned forward and said, "If you are right, it will turn archaeology in Jerusalem on its head."

However, when I read the following verses, our conversation took an even more exciting turn. First Kings 1:38-39: *"So Zadok the priest, Nathan the prophet, Benaiah the son of Jehoiada, the Cherethites and the Pelethites went down and had Solomon ride on King David's mule and took him to Gihon. Then Zadok, the priest took a horn of oil from the tabernacle and anointed Solomon...."*

Chuck was now gazing at the Bible verses on my cell phone and then lifted his head, "The Bible is actually saying here that Solomon was taken to the Gihon Spring and at that very spot the priest enters the tabernacle that held the Ark of the Covenant and gets oil to anoint the newly crowned king."

"That's absolutely right," I exclaimed. The tabernacle with the ark in its hold was at Gihon Spring in the City of David at Zion.

THE STRONGHOLD

Sensing Chuck's amiability on the theory, I went on to explain that I believe this event happened at the same Gihon Spring where David set the tent tabernacle in very close proximity to the threshing floor area.

David's tent stood for some 38 years housing the Ark of the Covenant until Solomon moved the ark up to his newly built temple, which was more than likely located side by side with the Ophel mound area at the Gihon Spring. The Ophel is translated in the King James Version as the *stronghold*, the same word used in 2 Samuel 5:7.[1]

It was there they offered sacrifices, the place that once was in the area of a threshing floor that separated wheat from chaff, and the place of a future temple where Jesus will rule and separate wheat (believers) from the chaff (non-believers). It was a precise place of holy destiny.

Chuck looked at me quizzically, as if he were gazing into my soul. I further explained that the Bible states that the City of David was also known as the place of the temple: *"Now Solomon brought the daughter of Pharaoh up from the City of David to the house he had built for her, for he said. 'My wife shall not dwell in the house of David king of Israel, because the places to which the ark of the Lord has come are holy'"* (2 Chronicles 8:11).

Biblical mandates kept lining up. Not only was the temple built on the threshing floor (see 2 Chronicles 3:1) within the walled confines of the city of David (which in no way can be at the traditional Temple Mount), it was specifically prepared as the landing place for the tabernacle as well, prior to Solomon's temple being erected. So the tent of David was set there (on the threshing floor) and each successive temple was also laminated over the same precise place.

I again stressed the importance to Chuck about the verse in 2 Samuel 5:7 that reads, *"Nevertheless, David took the stronghold of Zion (that is, the City of David)."* Then I offered the following in a more dogmatic pronouncement. Feeling a pit in my stomach, I said, "Since Scripture says that the temple is in Zion and Zion is in the City of David, then it is virtually impossible to have the temple located on the traditional Temple Mount/Dome of the Rock platform no matter how strong tradition says to the contrary."

At this moment, Dr. Missler looked at me and asked, "Do you even realize what you are saying here?" I stammered out a "Yes,"—my words carrying more conviction than my queasy stomach anticipated as to what he was about to say.

Chuck paused for a moment and said, "These facts are pretty surprising and revealing, even for an old Bible student like me."

He took a breath and resumed, "Just think of the implications for the temple being rebuilt off of the Muslim-controlled Temple Mount. He leaned forward, "What will it all mean for the events in the Middle East, and for Bible prophecy?" His bushy eyebrows furrowed: "Bob, do you realize this could change everything?"

THE REDISCOVERY OF ZION

Meeting Chuck lit a fresh fire in my heart to carry on, and so I kept studying Scripture, kept finding more and more clues, and discovered along the way a treasure chest full of exciting and revealing information.

I started in Psalm 48:9-13: *"We have thought, O God, on Your loving kindness, in the midst of Your temple. According to Your name, O God, so is Your praise to the ends of the earth; Your right hand is full of righteousness. Let Mount Zion rejoice, let the daughters of Judah be glad, because of Your judgments. Walk about Zion, and go all around her. Count her towers; mark well her bulwarks; consider her palaces; That you may tell it to the generation following."*

These verses are a deep well of knowledge; they lay out several significant strong points: Seaming them together they can be read as: God is in the temple, and Zion is the place of the temple, and we should remember the towers, palaces, and bulwarks of the City of David as a testimony for generations that will come after us.

To me, this final verse was possibly describing the time in which we are now living. We are one of those *generations that follow* and should use the testimony from God's accurate and trustworthy Words to take heed, no matter how popular, dogmatic, or how entrenched a contrary tradition has become.

The archaeological evidence is there, the Bible verses are there, the eyewitness testimony from history is there, yet acceptance of the temple being in the City of David (Zion) is considerably absent, thus the next generations need to be informed (as the above verse says), *"That you may tell it to the generation following"* that the temple is at Zion and that Zion is in the biblically established correct zone of the City of David's towers, walls and bulwarks. History demands this—and so does the Bible.

Zion is sacrosanct with the City of David and the temple. They are joined together in one location. But many are confused with the term Zion, and rightly so. As mentioned earlier, history has mangled the location because tradition has once again wrapped its tentacles around Zion and dragged it off to a wrong site. Without any geographical basis at all, fourth century writings, without any critical examination, erroneously proclaimed Zion to be located in the upper city area. This was a blunder of the ages—a mistaken placement of Zion which resulted in mass confusion as to the proper temple site.

From the years 1875 to 1888, Professor Birch from England rediscovered the real Zion at the lower edge of the southeast ridge in the City of David, but scholars not only seemingly ignored this, but they also still continue to defend the traditional Temple Mount location as the place of the temple.

Again, to further clarify the significance of Zion, 2 Chronicles 3:1 tells us: *"Now Solomon began to build the temple at the house of the Lord at Jerusalem...at the place that David had prepared on the threshing floor of Ornan the Jebusite."* The threshing floor, of course, was situated in the City of David which is undeniably the precise place of Zion. We know that Zion is in the City of David because Scripture states, *"Nevertheless David took the stronghold of Zion (that is, the City of David)"* (2 Samuel 5:7). So there is absolutely no doubt that David bought the threshing floor as a site to build a future temple and it was in the strict confines of the ancient outline walls of the City of David—which the Bible clearly refers to as the stronghold of Zion.

GOD'S "HOLY MOUNTAIN"

The City of David was rediscovered in the later 1800s and its walls begin at about 600 feet south of today's traditional Temple Mount/Dome of the Rock. I found that the Bible further states, *"So shall you know that I am the Lord your God, dwelling in Zion My holy mountain"* (Joel 3:7). This is reflective of the verse which reads, *"My holy mountain Jerusalem...as the children of Israel bring an offering in a clean vessel into the house of the Lord"* (Isaiah 66:20).

These verses indicate that "My holy mountain" is the same as "the House of the Lord," which is synonymous with the temple. Since the threshing floor is the site of the temple which is in the City of David as well as the true place of Zion, it seems all three converge and solidify in logical summation as well as logical submission that the true location of the temple needs to shift to its proper and original site—south of the traditional Temple Mount.

Micah 4:2-13 gives a further prophetic picture of the temple being located on the threshing floor in the City of David. From the Oxord Study Bible (OSB), let me seam several verses together to make that point.

> *In the days to come,*
> *The mountain of the Lord's house*
> *Will be established higher than all other mountains*
> *The Lord will bring their King on Mount Zion*
> *They do not know the Lord's thoughts or understand His purpose;*
> *For He has gathered them like sheaves to the threshing-floor*
> *Start your threshing you people of Zion.*

The *"Lord's house"* (as referenced above) is the temple itself. So we have another non-retractable connector with the temple, Zion, and the threshing floor.

Once again, the threshing floor (see 2 Chronicles 3:1) is all important in identifying the temple location. Its connection to Zion, in the City of David, adds to the corroborative evidence of the true temple location. But again, tradition is like a large cement mixer that drives through history, stopping over falsehoods that are convenient to the church at the time, and then dumping its contents. What we have years later is a hardened and unchallengeable shell that a pile-driver can't seem to break open.

But the Bible certainly can!

CHAPTER 8

THE FLOWING WATERS OF GIHON

In 1896, a treasure trove of old records were discovered in Cairo in what was referred to as a document cemetery. No bigger than a good-sized walk-in closet, the Genizah Documents were found moldering in their musty storage grave. They had sat there for many years, blanketed with specks of crumbling white roof plaster that had fallen on them like snowflakes from a decaying sky. Many claim this ancient, rare caché is second to only the Dead Sea Scrolls.

It was certainly a monumental discovery of ancient hidden Hebrew writings that Jews had refused to throw away. They were primarily important synagogue documents that had become unusable. But, because they had God's name on them, or they had just decayed to a point of uselessness, these hallowed records were stored in what is called a *genizah* (Hebrew for hiding place), and these storage places (sacred trash bins) were often found in old basements, hidden niches, or the attics of a synagogue.

The Genizah Documents indicate that seventh century Jews from Tiberius believed that the gates from the temple were *not* on the traditional Temple Mount but south of that location over the water system of the Spring of Gihon.

When the Caliph Omar visited Jerusalem shortly after the conquest, he asked the Jews, "Where would you wish to live in the city?" They answered, "In the Southern section of the city, which is the market of the Jews."[1]

The Jews, by saying this, wanted to be close to the real temple site and its gates, as well as the waters of Siloam [Gihon Spring]. These very rare and important written records make it clear that, at least in the seventh century, the Jews from Tiberius had gained knowledge which caused them to believe that the temple was situated contiguous to Gihon in the City of David and in the stronghold of Zion. They never fully accepted that the temple was on what we now call the Temple Mount.

THE RIGHT VIEWPOINT

When I was a police officer in California, I worked for a while as a motorcycle cop. One day I was riding behind a car that had a layer of bugs splattered all over the rear license plate. I could not imagine anyone driving in reverse at such a speed that it would cause bugs to accumulate as splattered insects on the rear plate. I stopped the car and found out it had been stolen. The suspect had taken the plates from a local car and, in his haste, the rear plate was put on the front and the front plate was carelessly placed on the rear of the vehicle.

If we look at the evidence, tilting it to the proper angle, no matter how insignificant it may seem, it can lead to surprising results. One small nugget of information that has huge implications is again from Josephus. For me, as a cop, it offers a clue like bugs on a license plate.

Flavius Josephus wrote that the temple could not even be seen from the north of the city of Jerusalem. This is a small indicator that has some scholars awkwardly baffled because if you stand in the north of the city and look to the south, as Josephus suggests, you will see the high stonewalls of the traditional Temple Mount/Dome of the Rock platform. This structure of great magnitude almost fills the horizon from the north vantage point and can be seen all the way to Ramallah.

So why does Josephus write that you *cannot* even see the temple from the north of the city? It is simple: the temple was on the other side (south) of the Dome of the Rock/Temple Mount platform nestled in the city of David. The real temple, in the lower elevation and the City of David, was blocked from view because the imposing Roman fort (Temple Mount) stood in the way.

That is why, from the north of Jerusalem, the entirety of the

Roman garrison shielded the sight of the temple from Josephus.[2]

That angle of view, like that on the vehicle plates, changed everything. The stolen car revealed a suspicious situation and the hidden truth was found simply because the right angle of sight was discovered.

The temple, not being seen from the north of Jerusalem may seem like a small detail, but it is a very powerful notation by Josephus because it completely destroys the idea that the Dome of the Rock platform could possibly be the correct placement of the former temple.

THE ARISTEAS ACCOUNT

I love eyewitnesses! There is nothing more dramatic during courthouse proceedings than when a witness raises a finger and points to the defendant and announces, "There he is. There is the person who committed the crime."

Another witness who points his finger to the Gihon Spring being located in the interior portion of the temple is a man named Aristeas, a visitor from Egypt who recorded a description of the temple and Jerusalem about fifty years after Alexander the Great. He was memorialized by Eusebius, who quoted him as observing, "There is an inexhaustible reservoir of water, as would be expected from an abundant spring gushing up naturally from within the [temple]."[3]

This prodigious water that was seen by Aristeas in the temple was witnessed long before the two aqueducts were built in the time of the Hasmoneans (the Maccabees) as well as Pilate, to channel water to Jerusalem from the south of Bethlehem.

Old Aristeas is pretty clear that a never-ending spring gushed from the temple confines, but since the Temple Mount has no spring at all, this ancient historical source needed dealing with from scholars who really have a problem with what Aristeas said. They also have difficulty with what Roman historian Tacitus wrote concerning a spring in the temple (which we will discuss in a moment).

These ancients were obviously referring to the Gihon Spring for the temple site, but again some scholars didn't like it because they did not want to suggest that the temple was anywhere off the Temple Mount. So some of these writers simply changed the words of Aristeas to read, *"just as if there were a plentiful spring..."*[4]

There is a big discrepancy between "there is a spring" and the inconclusive and diluting, "just as if there were a spring." This play on words seems to be an edit with the intention of making the temple location comply with the Dome of the Rock site for the temple. But whether editing history or editing the original meaning of the Bible, any alterations deflect ultimate truth and all we wind up with is a confusing hybrid of historical facts.

TACITUS, JOEL, AND THE SPRING

Tacitus, the Roman historian, is another witness who lifts a finger and points past the shadows of antiquity and into the heart of truth. He wrote roughly 400 years after Aristeas and recorded that the temple at Jerusalem had *a natural spring of water that welled from its interior.*[5]

Again, these references could only be describing the Gihon Spring. It is located close to what is referred to as the Ophel, which is a bulge of the earth abutting the City of David (Zion) laying just to the south, and roughly about 1,000 feet, from the Temple Mount.

There is no other such spring(s) anywhere else in Jerusalem. However, there is a place called the En-Rogel which is situated about a third of a mile southeast of the City of David, but this is not a spring at all, rather a well. The spring connection, especially a robust gushing spring, seems to be like a laser pointer aimed at the City of David and not at the Temple Mount as the temple site.

I stumbled across another fascinating verse that makes it irrefutable that a spring/fountain needs to be a fundamental component of the temple location: *"A fountain shall flow from the house of the Lord..."* (Joel 3:18). Can it be any clearer that a water source (spring/fountain) flows from the House of the Lord (temple) which held the Ark of the Covenant? This verse is more solidly dogmatic in its pronouncements because it says unequivocally that a spring flows from the temple.

The temple would logically need a prodigious amount of water (Gihon Spring) for cleaning up after all the animal blood sacrifices. Gihon Spring is the only spot that has enough water for the temple sacrifices in all of Jerusalem. It appears that the Roman garrison could not obtain water from this spring because it was holy water for temple usage. If the Romans even tried to take one drop, it would result in violent rioting, so they were forced to bring water from south of Bethlehem, as they did via aqueducts that fed the many underground cisterns storage at the purported fort.

If Joel 3:18 is not enough to convince you, there is another verse containing Zion in connection with a spring and the ark as well. The psalmist wrote, *"And of Zion it will be said... Both the singers and the players on instruments say, 'All my springs are within you.'"* (Psalm 87:5,7).

This verse has the words *singers and players on instruments* which is associated in the Bible with a processional carrying the ark (Psalm 68). The words *springs are within you* would be consistent with the Gihon Spring as well as the word *Zion,* which is connected with both the temple and the City of David.

DEAD SEA, LIVE WATER

Writings discovered on the Dead Sea Scrolls also describe a spring inside the temple. The Essenes living in the sun-blistered plateau by the Dead Sea wrote down on papyri what a shepherd would come to find in 1947. The crumbling clay jars held a two-thousand-year-old written record of events long ago and I visited those very same caves at Qumran where the papyri were found. It was July 2013, and in 104-degree heat, I sat staring at the famed cave entrance from across the narrow wadi. In my mind's-eye, I could almost visualize the searching shepherd back in 1947 as he tossed a stone in the cave looking for his lost sheep.

And then he heard it!

In the small mouth of the dark cave the sound of breaking clay jars echoed back to the shepherd's ears. It would turn out to be one of the greatest archaeological finds of all time.

One of the scrolls found had a temple description on disintegrating scraps of papyrus. Keep in mind that the men who wrote these scrolls knew full well about the temple precincts, which were still in existence prior to the temple's destruction in 70 AD. One scroll contained this instruction: *"You shall make a channel all-round the laver within the building. The channel runs* [from the building] *of the laver to a shaft, goes down and disappears in the middle of the earth so that the water flows and runs through it and is lost in the middle of the earth."*

This recorded message from the Dead Sea Scrolls plainly refers to the temple in relation to a tunnel system which is in the proximity of Gihon.[6]

EZEKIEL'S VISION

In the Bible there is yet another reference that was discovered with a secure connection to the Gihon Spring/temple correlation. It is found in Ezekiel 47:1-2: *"Then he brought me back to the door of the temple; and there was water, flowing from under the threshold of the temple faced east; the water was flowing from under the right side of the temple, south of the altar. He brought me out by way of the north gate, and led me around on the outside to the outer gateway that faces east; and there was water running out on the right side."*

This verse not only talks of water flowing from the temple but from south of the altar.

There are other Hebrew writings cited in a book by Zev Vilnay that also mention by name the Gihon Spring area as the place for the future temple. *"...At that time a great stream shall flow forth from the Holy Temple and its name is Gihon."* His book refers to Jewish writings that specifically declare that the Gihon Spring was where the high priest immersed in the spring's water. The special place was called the Bath of Ishmael and it was used for purification by the high priest on the Day of Atonement.[7]

THE CLEANSING STREAM

Because of all the blood sacrifices, the temple was an absolute bloody mess. Solomon sacrificed *twenty-two thousand bulls and one hundred and twenty thousand sheep* when he dedicated the temple (1 Kings 8:62). With so many animals being slaughtered, the severed veins would spray blood like a cut garden hose. There were thirteen tables in the temple, with eight marble slabs in the slaughter house.[8]

There would be so much blood that the red-clotted rivulets would need to go somewhere, and the only place was down some sort of a drainage canal which I would later get to explore—underground, in the area south of the Temple Mount.

The only thing available in ancient times to wash clean all that blood was water, and lots of it. If the blood was left standing, it would become putrefied, creating a disease-spreading disaster. There absolutely had to be a robust water source to wash away all the waste.

The Gihon Spring is the only possible scenario for those water needs. The Gihon was the place where the tabernacle containing the ark was located when Solomon was crowned (1 Kings), and this gurgling water became a nexus of historical and biblical pronouncements that it was indeed a key feature of the temple site.

It has been said that High Priest Rabbi Yishmael from the second temple period used the Gihon as a ritual bath for purification prior to entering the temple: "Near there is a cave. People go down to it by stairs. It is full of pure water, and there is a tradition that it is the ritual bath of Rabbi Yshmael the High Priest." (as quoted in the name of Rabbi Moshe, in: Moshe Ben Menachem Mendl Reicher, Sharrei Yerushalayim Shar`ar 8.33).

It is interesting that a second temple period arch has been found above a stone staircase descending to the Gihon Spring, giving evidence that the spring was in service at the time of Herod's temple. It was surmised in the book, *The City of David,* written by Ahron Horovitz (p. 213), that the spring served as an entranceway to those coming to purify themselves at the time of the second temple era. If this were the case, then a huge question begs asking: *if priests and people purified themselves at the Gihon Spring prior to entering the temple, why would they then walk almost a quarter mile to the traditional Temple Mount area?*

That trek of distance and likely human/animal interaction would make them unclean and unworthy to enter any temple precincts. It would be like a doctor scrubbing up for surgery and then walking a quarter of a mile on dusty streets as well as coming in contact with unwashed contaminants along the way. Doctors would not do this and priests, in their holy duties at the temple, would not be purified in the waters of the Gihon only to later comingle with potential sullying elements.

The Gihon was the running subterranean river that washed the priests to a pure state so they would not go anywhere afterwards other than to immediately enter, without any divergence, directly into the temple compound.

Even as far back as Moses and the time of the tabernacle, spring water was essential in the purification ceremony for priests. Josephus writes in *Jewish Antiquities* (Book 3,8.6), "Moses had sprinkled Aaron's vestments, himself, and his sons, with the blood of the beasts that were killed, and had purified them with spring water and ointment, they became God's priests."

Spring water (moving pure water) and ointments (olive oil) were absolute essential needs for purification rituals. The only running water in the desert that was available to Moses was the water from the split rock—and the only spring water available in Jerusalem was the Gihon Spring, which was in the City of David, within the stone wall boundaries of the stronghold of Zion.

PIECING THE CLUES TOGETHER

So the next big pin that needs to be stuck on the map as the correct temple site should be over the spring of Gihon. Its location is referred to numerous times in the book of Psalms and by the prophets. The Gihon Spring, during the times of David and Solomon, supplied water for the Pool of Siloam. Also, King

Hezekiah carved out a tunnel to move underground water from the Gihon Spring to western Jerusalem in anticipation of a siege against Jerusalem by Assyrian King Sennacherib (2 Chronicles 32:30).

It would be this subterranean water source that would offer a major clue for the true temple location. It seems the spring has been gurgling with whispered shouts for a very long time now and, obviously, we have not been listening.

There comes a time in every investigation when you realize that your findings are probably going to convince a jury. But even though the evidence is sound and logical, there is always the chance your case will fall like a deck of cards. That is the nature of any jury decision; it is often carried on the whims of personal belief.

For me, the Gihon, Zion, and the City of David all seem interrelated, like next of kin who have a strong family tree that is old and scarred by age, but anchored deep with eternal roots.

Chapter 9

The Apostle's Arrest

In writing one of my previous books, *The Lost Shipwreck of Paul*, I spent years researching this amazing man. Most of the time he seems to be involved in some kind of trouble, and always at the center of action.

In Acts 21, he is the focus of the story once again: Paul entered the temple in Jerusalem after having publicly fraternized with his "unclean Gentile friends." Upon hearing that Paul had walked into this sacred compound with his *filthy* friends in tow, the local people quickly formed a mob and descended on the temple complex.

Once inside, the irate throng grabbed Paul and dragged him out of the gate, beating him with the intent to kill. As news of the angry rioters reached the Roman commander in the garrison, the officer rushed with a company of soldiers to take control of the situation.

At that point, something took place that really grabbed my attention. I read in Acts 21:32. The Roman commander ... ***"immediately took soldiers and centurions**, and ran **down** to them."* (emphasis mine) This verse tells us that the Roman soldiers went *down* to get Paul.

This should raise a significant red flag for anyone believing in the Temple Mount because it is a high-walled fortress-looking edifice. You can only go down from there. If The Temple Mount was the place of Paul's riot scene, then the big question is where would someone go down *from* to reach Paul. There would have to be a fort floating somewhere in the clouds to match the biblical account. And it is even more interesting later in verse 35, where it reads that when Paul reached the stairs he had to be carried *up* by the soldiers. So, according to the Bible, we have to have stairs descending from the Roman garrison to the lower temple gates and then they had to carry Paul going back up into the Roman garrison (traditional Temple Mount platform). This can only apply if the temple, for instance, is in the old City of David in the area of the Gihon Spring.

Now if Paul was taken up the southern side of the Temple Mount, what has archaeology found there? Roman memorabilia has been unearthed all over the area. For instance, a huge broken column honoring Vespasian was discovered south of the southern wall of the Temple Mount. The column had the inscription ending with the line...*the Tenth Legion Pretenses.*[1]

And what other artifacts have archaeologists uncovered by that "stair area" south of the Dome of the Rock, where I surmise Paul was taken up the stairs to the Roman fort? They have collected 240 fragments of broken bricks stamped with the words...*Tenth Roman Legion.*[2]

In the book by Dr. Eilat Mazar, *The Complete Guide to the Temple Mount Excavations*, she says, "The exact location of the Tenth Legion camp in Jerusalem is subject to debate. The section of the camp wall, the public buildings, and the numerous finds associated with the Tenth Legion found in the excavations indicate that the camp occupied the area at the foot of the southwestern corner of the temple mount enclosure, as well as, apparently, the Temple Mount itself."

Evidently, enough evidence has been unearthed to justify such a statement.

THE GARRISON

If the Roman garrison occupied the 36 acre Temple Mount of today, then some rather dramatic events took place there—one being the arrest of Paul and the other the arrest of Christ. The brutal treatment of Jesus is well recognized, but Paul's arrest is less known. The apostle was once a devout Jew who persecuted Christians mercilessly. According to Scripture, Christians questioned his sincerity when Paul eventually professed to have a dramatic conversion to the faith. Then, when Paul preached Jesus as *Messiah*, his old cronies and the Jewish Pharisees as well, stamped him as a lunatic traitor to their faith. They could not stomach the fact that an executed criminal, named Jesus, could have so many followers years after his execution; and then, in the type of inexplicable turnabout that made their blood boil, Paul himself, their lead prosecutor of Christians, had converted, too. It most certainly filled them with a disgust that, on a smaller scale, exceeded their hatred of the Romans, who still occupied their land.

No one could have confronted the depths of their religious hypocrisy like this formerly high-ranking Jew named Saul (now named Paul), preaching a new religion concerning the Man whom he talked about as being the "Son of God." Plainly put, Paul had committed national treason because of his new belief, and they vowed to get rid of him.

THE NECESSITY OF A LARGE FORT

As stated before, when Paul entered the temple in Jerusalem, and after publicly fraternizing with unclean Gentiles, a mob was quickly formed and descended on the temple complex. Once inside, the angry crowd seized Paul and dragged him out the gates, beating him with the intent to take his life. As news of the disturbance reached the Roman commander, the officer went from the fort and down the steps with a company of soldiers to confront the irate crowd waiting at the temple gate.

After quieting the riot, the Roman guards bound Paul in chains and took him up the stairs to the barracks of Fort Antonia. The commander of the Roman forces in Judea saw no reason for a trial for this Jewish troublemaker: a major disturbance had erupted in the streets of Jerusalem and Paul was clearly to blame. He would be beaten until he either confessed or died.

A soldier stood near Paul and tensed his grip around the whip, a menacing ensemble of leather blood-stained thongs interwoven with jagged pieces of metal and bone. But, before the centurion could administer this patently Roman form of justice, Paul lifted his bloody, swollen face and sternly inquired, "Is it lawful for you to scourge a man who is a Roman and uncondemned?"

The soldier's outstretched arm slowly dropped to his side, the whip dangling in the dirt. He looked to the centurion, who stood speechless. "This Jewish prisoner has just claimed to be a citizen of Rome," the centurion said. And with that, Paul's destiny changed.

For a Jew in Roman Judea, it was nothing unusual to be dragged to jail, accused of being a suspicious Jew, and then pummeled and lashed into expected submission. But to flog a *citizen* of Rome, especially without a trial or legal condemnation, was strictly forbidden. The centurion confronted the commander and asked, "What are you going to do? This man is a Roman citizen."

The commander bent down toward Paul. "Are you a citizen of Rome?" he asked. "Yes," Paul replied.

Shocked, the commander probed further to see if his prisoner was simply a wealthy Jew who had bribed his way to a privileged position. The officer admitted, *"With a large sum I obtained this citizenship."*

Paul replied, *"But I was born a citizen"* (Acts 22:28).

Alarmed at realizing he had put a Roman citizen in chains, the commander contemplated his next move and ordered Paul to be untied. The next morning, hoping to clear up what had become a confusing mess, the commander instructed all the chief priests and their council to appear before him. Minutes later Paul stood before the crowd to give an account of himself. *"Men and brethren,"* he began, *"I have lived in all good conscience before God until this day"* (Acts 23:1).

Even this basic claim so incensed the high priest that he ordered Paul hit about the mouth. Spitting blood, Paul shot back, (saying in essence) "You hit me without reason, you hypocrite. You sit and judge me, and you strike without me being charged, so you're the one who breaks the law."

By the end of the meeting, another furious mob had tried to wring Paul's neck. Once again, the soldiers had to drag him to safety. Paul was later forced to appear in Rome, and would continue to contend with brazen threats against his life—in one case narrowly escaping a clandestine plot by forty men, bound with an oath to neither eat or drink until Paul was dead.

Ultimately, two hundred soldiers, seventy horsemen, and two hundred spearmen accompanied Paul on his way to Caesarea, illustrating just how great a sensation this story had become in the middle of the first century Roman world.

Paul was big news, already renowned among believers in that region—many of whom believed that even the handkerchiefs and garments Paul touched would heal the sick. And now his peculiar fame had spread across the empire, triggering deep, passionate emotions in everyone who heard his story.

In Caesarea, Paul fell under the jurisdiction of Felix, a former slave himself, who rose (with the help of some strategic marriages) to become Governor of Judea. A greedy, horrible man, Felix let his famous prisoner sit in jail, hoping to collect a substantial bribe. The result being that Paul languished in a dungeon prison for two more years. So the apostle's story gives us two huge clues as to the temple location.

To recap the situation, after his arrest at the temple, Paul was taken up the stairs of the Roman fort, which could only mean that he was in a lower elevation at the temple gate. That fits perfectly with the lower city of David location for the temple to the south, and an elevated Roman fort to the north (traditional Temple Mount).

It would also mean that there was some distance between the temple and the Roman Fort Antonia. Again, those soldiers went down the stairs to get Paul as they proceeded to retrieve him at the temple gate. This seems to completely discount the popular Avi-Yonah model found today at the Israeli museum because that model shows the temple and the Roman Fort Antonia as being conjoined to each other.

Paul was escorted to Caesarea by 470 soldiers after his arrest. This means that the Roman fort needed to be much larger than many scholars suggest. A fort that could easily spare 470 soldiers for only one man had to be at least the size of a legion with support personnel totaling around ten thousand people. The idea that a small fort was all there was in Jerusalem to control the often riotous Jews is illogical. The temple mount is the perfect size for the Roman fort needs. Also, the thought that the Temple Mount had stairs descending from a phantom fort floating in the air above is equally illogical.

So Paul's arrest gives us more evidence regarding the location of the temple.

CHAPTER 10

A VALLEY OF BLOOD

A family friend of ours and fellow researcher, Rhonda Sand, told me that she was one of the first to tour a large drainage ditch coming from the Temple Mount area which dated to the time of the Roman occupation. She logically assumed that it was waste flowing from the temple because the large underground stone-lined tunnel started at the southwest corner of the Temple Mount platform and headed south down to the southern tip of the City of David to the valley below. I started planning a trip because I wanted to find out what this huge drainage ditch might have to do with the temple being at the Gihon Spring.

After a few days in Jerusalem, researching and conducting interviews, I decided to spend a day in the ancient underground sewer trench area. It was smelly, wet, mossy, dank, but it was also well lit. At some places, it is a bit tight and in others it is spaciously wide, spanning six or more feet. The ceiling heights varied from decent to one requiring me to bend over just to get through.

Halfway into the tunnel I stopped to take in the moment. Most would not have a visceral flash of reflection in an ancient sewer tunnel, but I knew what had happened here almost two thousand years ago. I could almost hear the echoed screams of those who fled the Romans en masse and hid away in these very tunnels.

The rocks above me showed evidence of being smashed downward in a few places. The Romans had slaughtered countless thousands in the city above in the great revolt, and many survivors fled to the sewer channels, carrying food in pots that were later found by archaeologists. The Romans eventually caught them all and it was a bloodbath.

In Josephus, (*Wars*, 6,9,4) we read, "The Romans slew many of them, some they carried captives, and others made a search for the underground, and when they [the Romans] found where they were, they broke up the ground and slew all that they met with."

As I walked through the long channel, I saw hard-hat workers removing rocks and earth from a side tunnel. The smell of dirt breathing air for the first time in two thousand years greeted me and it was a good aroma coming over the old dank smell of the place. I ventured past the DO NOT ENTER sign and a worker identified himself as Nissim Mizrachi, the digging and discoveries administrator. He had a hearty smile framed with a bushy long gray beard that held a dusting of dirt.

"No admission," he said, "you could get hurt." Just then a rock the size of a basketball rolled to my feet from the work area. Nissim said nothing. He didn't have to. I backed off with a sincerely sorry expression. He turned to walk away, having made his point, but I followed him, almost pestering him with rapid fire questions.

I felt it fortuitous to meet in the very place I had come so far to visit. He just kept moving down the tunnel with a stocky-framed trudge, then turned, "Why are you so interested in an ancient sewer?" he asked with inquisitive eyes.

I told him, "I have traveled from America just to see this place.

He sniffed the air and made an unpleasant expression, "To an old sewer you come?"

"Yes," I said. I think at that moment he became more interested in the situation than me. He smiled then asked me, "What is it you want?"

I replied, "Where does this ancient sewer go? Where does it come from?"

He said, "It comes from up there," and he lifted a stub of a finger pointing up the shaft and then swivelled his arm toward the opposite direction and said, "it goes down there."

I asked "Does it come from the Temple Mount?"

He paused, "It starts at the southwest corner of the Temple Mount."

My enthusiasm sank. I had hoped that the sewer was the channel that came from the Ophel area by the spring of Gihon. I thought a moment and realized that if the Temple Mount was the location of a Roman garrison that housed about nine thousand or more people, which is the size of a small city, it would certainly need a channel to wash away all that human waste and garbage. I then thought, if this was for the garrison, then maybe there were similar channels running from the direction of the suspected temple area close to the Gihon Spring that might carry blood waste from all the many animal sacrifices.

I asked my newly-acquainted bearded friend if such channels even existed. He slowly raised his finger up to his lips and made a "shuuusssh" sound as he looked around trying to see if anyone else was listening.

"Why do you ask such a thing?" he said; his words now flat. I told him I thought the temple of Solomon and Herod were somewhere in the area of the Gihon Spring.

There was an awkward silence when he uttered nothing, but stared at me from eyes darting about. He turned and said, "Follow me."

SECRETS OF THE SEWER

We stepped through puddles of mud and past slimy green walls. He was a wide man, but he maneuvered through the narrow spaces with the ease of a cat. He stopped suddenly, and then in an almost diving motion entered head long into a stone-lined chamber of about two feet by three feet wide. He held a red laser pointer in his right hand and craned his neck for me to look past him. His legs dangled from the opening and I moved to his side to look. It was an unexcavated tunnel leading directly to the area of the Gihon Spring.

His grunting voice echoed in the stone canal, "We haven't been down there yet, but we will tunnel back once we get some other digging done first." He wiggled out and then it was my turn, and I wiggled in. It was so beautiful, such a lovely site considering the burgeoning theory. It was lined all around on all four sides with tight-fitting flat stones that had been hand chiseled to perfection. How could I be so fortunate to find this man at this place at this moment?

Was I looking at a canal that carried the blood from the temple of Solomon?

"There are three more of these canals in the drainage/sewer channel coming from the same direction of the Gihon," Nissim said slowly, as if he was pondering the possibility as well. My mind whirled.

Could these ancient stone-encased channels actually be from the temple area by the Gihon, and did they carry the blood from its confines? Ezekiel foretold of a future temple that described tables for sacrificing. Though not Solomon's or Herod's temples, this prophetic temple was depicted as having slaughtering tables: *"At the outer side of the vestibule, as one goes up to the entrance of the northern gateway, were two tables; and on the other side of the vestibule of the gateway were two tables. Four tables were on this side and four tables on that side, by the side of the gateway, eight tables on which they slaughtered the sacrifices"* (Ezekiel 40:40-41).

So when Nissim talked about the four channels which had been found, my mind went into dizzying overload.

The man leaned over, and with a big grin, whispered, "It was in this area that I found the famous gold bell."

I had read about the gold bell. It was thought to have fallen from a temple priest's robe. As I stood where the two channels met, I could only wonder: Had that gold bell come from the wide Temple Mount channel or was it from one of the four channels leading from the Gihon and the site of the lost temple?

I will never know, but I did know one thing for sure about the temple precincts prior to the temple's destruction in 70 AD. As mentioned before, the Dead Sea Scrolls had a message from long ago, "You shall make a channel all-round the laver within the building. The channel runs [from the building] of the laver to a shaft, goes down and disappears in the middle of the earth so that the water flows and runs through it and is lost in the middle of the earth."[1]

I remembered that Aristeas, a half century after Alexander the Great, and Tacitus three centuries later, said that these springs were found only in the precincts of the temple.

I also recalled that the Gihon was a ritual bath for the high priest as was stated by Vilnay. It was in the Gihon that on the day of atonement the high priest would immerse himself before entering the Holy of Holies in the temple. The ritual bath was understood to be in the temple courtyard and from an earlier time, the Gihon was known as the *"Spring of the High Priest."*

Philo of Alexandria, a Jewish philosopher during the Roman control of Israel, called the spring, "the high priest's fountain" that carries off water—and also says that the water from this fountain channels underground, *"the pipes pour forth."*

Pipes are not necessarily like the pipes we have today that are round with threaded fittings, but a clay or stone-encased channel to remove waste-water that I believe was used in the slaughtering of many animals during blood sacrifices at the temple. Again, this temple was located at Gihon, at Zion in the City of David, and not on the traditional Temple Mount.

The large drainage ditch I first walked through, I began to believe, was to accommodate waste from the soldiers at the Antonia garrison. And all the blood run-off from the temple slaughtering of animals for sacrifice would eventually become joined in convergence in this huge drainage channel, and then, together, become the waste which was eventually dumped into the south valley at the low end of the City of David. A valley the locals still call today...*the valley of the blood.*

THE CHAMBER OF GEMARIAH

In July 2013, I returned to Jerusalem with my research team, which included Bonnie Dawson from Los Angeles and Dr. Paul Feinberg, a geologist and adjunct professor at Hunter College in New York. Both were excellent biblical researchers. Bonnie has a bright awareness of prophecy and Dr. Paul knows biblical history, geology, and geography. They were a terrific help in this most complex subject matter. I went over my findings and reports and they were most eager to get into the tunnels and ruins in and around the Gihon Spring.

The Israel Nature and Parks Authority operates an excellent

tour of the City of David area that includes Warren's shaft, the Gihon Spring, Hezekiah's Tunnel, the newly opened drainage channel as well as other sites and ruins. Bonnie and Dr. Paul seemed to center their initial interest on the *House of Bullae*. It was here in these ruins right next to the area of the Gihon Spring where something happened that archaeologists only dream about. We were in "Area G," which is a famous site within the City of David Excavation area where Yigal Shilo found a large collection of clay impressions (bulla).

In ancient times, when important documents were written on parchment or papyrus and the author wanted confidentiality, he would roll up the document and then put a stamp on the string that tied it up. This stamp was a round clay seal of sorts that had the impression pressed into it. In the case of the bulla found at this location, they had all been subjected to fire in a first temple period building where my research friends and I were standing. The fascinating thing was that the bulla had an inscription of a name we can accurately trace and link directly to the Bible and the temple.

Dr. Paul explained to me that the name *Gemariah son of Shapan* that was stamped on the bulla was the very Shapan who was the high official in the royal court. He was the person who read the scrolls to King Josiah, initiating temple reforms that had been lost (2 Kings 22:8). Shapan's son, Gemariah, had his name stamped on the clay bulla that somehow survived all this time.

It was here that Dr. Paul read from Jeremiah 36:10: *"Then Baruch read from the book the words of Jeremiah in the house of the Lord, in the chamber of Gemariah the son of Shapan the scribe, in the upper court at the entry of the New Gate of the Lords House..."*

Paul paused, then looked at me with a riveting stare, "Bob, do you think we are at the place of the chamber of Gemariah in the temple?" He rubbed some beads of sweat swelling on his forehead and swallowed dry. "These are ruins that archaeologists have yet to identify, and when they do, I think they will find this very place is the upper court at the New Gate."

I caught Bonnie looking down at the place that the bulla was found with Gemariah's name and she had the same stare, as if she agreed. Bonnie looked up at the both of us with her trademark whimsical smile and said, "All this research and evidence seems to be changing everything. I get chills thinking we are standing where the temple once stood."

I gazed down with a net full of verses swarming in my mind. This was the City of David; this was the original Zion, which is right over the unseen Gihon Spring that gushed below where we were standing. The moment seemed to be clarifying; the *bulla* discovered right here had the name *of Gemariah the son of Shapan the scribe, in the upper court at the entry of the New Gate of the Lords House...*

Could it be, as Dr. Paul suggested, that this was Gemariah's very chamber in *the House of the Lord* at the Gihon Spring? As I said before, there are no secrets that time and the Bible will not reveal. Yet, as astonishing as this bulla find is, there are other biblical names connecting to the temple that have been found in the ruins at or immediately around the Gihon Spring. For example, an unusual black stone with the name *Temech* inscribed upon it was also discovered in recent excavations and the book of Nehemiah tells us that the Temech family were servants of the ...*the first temple!*

The uncovered evidence was speaking volumes.

CHAPTER 11

DIGGING FOR ANSWERS

The question has been raised over and over again: *how was it possible to forget the location of the temple?*

Well, we did. And here are the reasons.

The Jews were removed from the land of Israel for very long periods of time. The years between 1150 AD and 1875 AD became known as the separation period. For 725 long years there were no scholars to speak of and no religious authorities having open access to the temple area. Any serious investigation was abandoned and, in time, anything that stagnates dies and is eventually erased from memory.

In addition, far too many eyewitnesses worthy of notation were slaughtered by the Romans leaving untold messages from the past precariously forgotten.

- We forgot because the temple was completely and utterly ripped from the earth like a tree plucked from the soil —roots and all.
- We forgot because Romans, after Herod the Great, and Muslims would not allow even a hint of a discussion with Jews to rebuild any temple.
- We forgot because people back then did not see a biblical event as something that needed memorializing. It was not important to them to make sure that a *place* was venerated; instead, they wanted to celebrate what *occurred* and what was *said* there.

This is why we have no conclusive evidence where Jesus once placed His foot, where He was crucified, or where He was buried. However we do have supreme records of those historic and often epic happenings, but frustratingly we have only scant geographical markers that can be assigned to those events.

Roman Emperor Hadrian (117-138 AD) rebuilt the destroyed city of Jerusalem, renamed it Aelia Capitolina, and kept Jews from entering. From the time of the Roman Emperor Julian the Apostate (middle of the fourth century) until the Arabs conquered Jerusalem in 638 AD, the Temple Mount had remained an abandoned garbage dump.[1]

The Crusaders later seized the Holy City in 1099 and placed a huge gilt cross on the famed Muslim Dome and called it *"Templum Domini"* (The Lord's Temple).

Because of this, a tradition was born!

TIME IS CRUEL TO TRUTH

In the twelfth century, the Muslims took the Dome of the Rock back and drove out the Christians. They put the crescent symbol of Islam back atop the Dome where it still sits today. The message all of this sends is that there have been huge spans of centuries where Romans kicked out Jews and Christians from the land, as well as Muslims enacting quarantine on Jews and Christians. During those long periods of conquest, the Temple Mount, as well as the City of David, were often lonely, forsaken places that knew only the stench of decaying trash or the sound of wind sifting through bent weeds.

Time is often cruel to truth, and abandonment stretching into centuries is the most unkind of all in attempting to locate where things once happened. The obscuring elements are like a lingering thick fog to a sailor alone at sea, lost without a compass. But fortunately, we *do* have a compass, and it is true and accurate.

When it says in Joel 3:17-18, *"So you shall know that I am the Lord your God dwelling in Zion My holy mountain...A fountain shall flow from the house of the Lord,"* it leaves us with clarion clues that allow us to know where to look for the lost temple. It is not on a high stone-walled plateau with a golden domed Muslim shrine topped with a crescent moon.

We need to turn our sight to an old Jebusite fortress known as the stronghold of Zion. For it is there that a spring pours forth prodigiously and that spring is called Gihon, which once flowed from the house of the Lord and will one day surge again from the Temple of God.

So back to the question: *how did we forget the location of the temples?* It is not uncommon that famed and endearing sites are lost to memory, because of eroding elements and civilizational progress. That was the case of Jamestown, which is so prominent in America's earliest chapters of European transplanted existence. In May 1607, a group of approximately 100 members of a joint venture known as the Virginia Company established the first permanent English settlement in North America. They decided to build a fort on the banks of the James River, on the southern fringe of the Chesapeake Bay. It was marshy, mosquito ridden, and had poor drinking water. By September of that year, half of them where dead, and by 1610, they were eating mice, rats, cats, and dogs just to survive. In time they would consume everything from shoe leather to their own dead. Jamestown somehow grew through the loss of life and with the help of some thriving crops such as tobacco, more settlers followed. From 1619 until 1621, 3,572 new immigrants aboard forty two ships came to Virginia.[2]

Even though a shocking number of them would die from disease, the darkened shadow of death could not stop growth; it seldom does. During the 1620s, Jamestown expanded from the original fort enclosure into a new town built just to the east. In 1698, the statehouse there burned. After that, the capitol was then moved eight miles inland to what we know today as Williamsburg.

Over the years Jamestown was long forgotten, consumed by the elements. Erosion had eaten away at the river banks and the neck of land connecting the mainland was submerged under the sluggish river currents making the forgotten Jamestown an Island. The exact location of Jamestown was lost, and no one knew where it was located. This most important piece of our national history was gone, vanished, a ghost fort hidden away among a tangle of thicket and the canopy of trees. But in 1994, archaeologists conclusively found the lost fort of Jamestown. And so, we have once again uncovered a very important place that had gone missing after only a few centuries. This leads us to ask again...*how could we forget God's holy mountain, which undoubtedly is the temple?*

We did! *"But you are those who forsake the Lord, who forget My holy mountain"* (Isaiah 65:11).

THE ISSUE OF ELEVATION

If the two colonnade bridges described by Josephus and interpreted as such by Dr. Martin that span horizontally level, then the temple in the City of David would need to be much higher. This might pose a problem for some.

But, if we examine some interesting clues, it is not a problem of compatible elevations at all. Barnabas said, fifteen years after the Jewish wars, that the temple was a tower.[3]

Josephus describes the eastern temple walls (down to the deep cut of the Kidron Valley) as exceeding *"all descriptions and words"* and that these high walls of the temple foundation were *"the most prodigious work that was ever heard of by man."*[4]

In addition, Josephus said that the foundation walls of the temple were of *"immense depths" and could be "hardly believed."* Therefore, it is understood that descriptions of the temple walls according to Barnabas formed a tower-looking edifice and, as stated by Josephus, the temple platform was remarkable in height but it still had to be much lower than the dome of the rock platform which dominated the skyline above. In the book by archaeologist Eilat Mazar, *The Discovery of the Menorah Treasure at the Foot of the Temple Mount,* (Shoham Academic Research, 2013), she describes the Ophal as the high area that had to be ascended (le-ha'apil).

Zion had some significant height assigned to it in the Bible as well. The east-west ridge does have an elevation rising majestically from the Kidron Valley, but lofty height would not be my definition. We might, however, have an explanation for that elevation quandary. It seems a man named Simon the Hasmonean is said by Josephus (*Antiquities XIII*, 6,7) to have had the ambitious project of working both day and night in removing some prominent elevation from the citadel [of David]. Simon, in essence, wanted to level the hill, so that the temple might be higher. This would explain the reduction of height expressed concerning Zion.

Josephus makes mention that the foundation walls of the temple went all the way down to the floor of the Kidron Valley, which would be on the east side of the temple. The height of the temple platform also seems to explain a potential difficult alliance with 2 Chronicles 5:2, where it says the ark was brought *up* by Solomon from the City of David and placed in the temple. The word *up* here simply means that the ark was carried to a higher position from the Gihon Spring to a taller structure which the temple certainly was (1 Kings 1:38-39). The caution here, however, is that Solomon's temple profile and elevation was probably different from Herod's temple (which Barnabas and Josephus were mentioning).

Yet, no matter how we grapple with uncertain prepositions, the Bible makes it very clear that Zion is where the temple should be, because God is described as *"dwelling in Zion"* (Psalm 9:11; 76:2). Also Psalm 65:1-4 clearly places God's temple *"in Zion."* And Psalm 99:1-2 enthrones God between the cherubim, which is *"in Zion."* In addition, Joel 3:17 and 21 put the temple squarely *"in Zion,"* which can only be located in the City of David and not on any tragically misdiagnosed Temple Mount locale.

Besides the biblical pronouncements of Zion as the bulls-eye for the temple, I need to mention again that Eusebius, one of the greatest and renowned historians of all time, makes this claim as well. He wrote, *"The hill called Zion and Jerusalem, the building there, that is to say, the temple, the Holy of holies..."*

Adding to the controversy surrounding the temple elevation and location is an Israeli architect in Tel Aviv, Tuvia Sagiv. His interesting observations are based on height and angle of sight and elevations found in historical accounts of King Herod Agrippa.

I am not an architect and have no way of verifying his claims; however, Sagiv is an expert in his field and has conducted extensive research of the Temple Mount area and has calculated its angles and datings. He writes the following in relation to the view that King Herod Agrippa had into the Temple based upon Flavius Josephus.

> *"...Agrippa built a huge hole in his palace...The palace had belonged to the Hasmonean family and was built on a high place. The king was able to observe from the palace what was happening in the temple. The people of Jerusalem objected to this because it was not the tradition to observe what was taking place in the temple, especially the animal sacrifices. Consequently, they built a high wall in the inner court above the western arcade...."*

So what did Agrippa actually see?

According to Tuvia Sagiv, Herod Agrippa's palace was west of the Temple Mount, at or near the present day Citadel and Jaffa Gate. "The altar in the temple cannot be directly seen looking from the west because the temple building prevents any view. The only way to see something going on in the Temple Courts is through the passageways between the temple wall and the walls of the court. If we were high enough, from the north we could see into the sacrifice-slaughter area, and viewing from the south we could see the altar's ramp. Moreover, without knowing exactly the location of Herod Agrippa's palace, using vertical sections, we discovered that the western court wall prevented any view from the western court, even without the addition of walls. In order to have seen what went on in the court, a building whose height was 31-47 meters above the ground (10-16 floors) was needed. Without mechanical equipment it would have been very difficult to climb to such a height, especially when concerning a building whose purpose was domestic and residential. Even from the highest towers in Jerusalem, the Phasael and Hippicus Towers, there was no way to see what was being done in the temple court during the time of the Second Temple. The height of these towers was 70-90 cubits, approximately 35-45 meters."[5]

Tuvia Sagiv concluded that both Agrippa's horizontal and vertical angles of sight prove that it is impossible to locate the Holy of Holies or the altar in the region of the Dome of the Rock.

A PERFECT FIT

Another challenge is that some say that there is not enough room in the City of David for the temple as compared to the huge traditional Temple Mount complex. It is also interesting that the Jewish Mishnah records that the temple should be on thirteen and a quarter acres—which fits perfectly with the City of David. The Dome of the Rock platform is thirty-six acres.

In the Middot, which means dimensions, or measurements, and thought to be the oldest portions of the Mishnah, it gives a square shape for the temple compound which included flanking rooms and courtyards. This involves a measurement of 500 cubits on each side.[6]

Josephus also confirms (in *War* V.5,2) that the temple was square-shaped. The traditional Temple Mount/Dome of the Rock platform however is not square at all, but a trapezium that measures 1,041 feet on its north wall, 1,596 feet on its west wall, 929 feet on its south wall and 1,556 feet on the east wall.

As mentioned earlier, Eusebius, the curator of the Library at Caesarea in the later third and early fourth centuries, wrote of the devastation of the temple at Sion (Zion), and all traces of it had been removed. Eyewitness testimony confirms this. The Roman fort was, however, still standing with its huge surrounding walls.

Yet, the Edict of Milan in 313 AD by Constantine and Licinuis, gave Jews the right to *"build the Lord's houses."*[7]

Where were they allowed to build? In the area of the Gihon Spring.

CHAPTER 12

THE DISCOVERY OF THE POOL OF SILOAM

In the fall of 2013, I felt that I had almost enough evidence for this book to be finalized. I had sent the rough manuscript to a list of scholars and pastors whose opinion I trust and was surprised by a vast majority of encouraging responses relating to the new temple theory. Many were not only accepting of the facts of the new temple site, they were enthusiastically supportive.

Around that time I received a call from Retired U.S. Army Brigadier General Norm Andersson who had read this manuscript. He told me that he had recently met with professor Chuck Benson, an esteemed architectural historian. Benson was in the process of drawing a cathedral in Mexico. Norm sent me some copies of Chuck's drawings and I was very impressed with his work. A meeting was set and I told Chuck at that time that I needed a set of various drawings of the temple mount as illustrations. He agreed on the spot to do them, and another team was assembled to head back to Jerusalem for one last search of the sites and to get the maps and drawings we needed for this book.

DOWN ANCIENT PASSAGEWAYS

On November 13, 2013, the team arrived in Jerusalem. That night in my hotel room, I was awakend from my sleep by an unmistakable sound. I opened my hotel window and looked into a black sky that was was smeared with an outstretched awning of sapphire stars. A lone, slender minaret rising from the flat rooftops emanated a melodic crackling sound that scratched away the still silence of a cool Israeli night. It was the Muslim call to prayer reverberating across the city. I knew that in that early hour, many Muslims were bowing in supplication towards Mecca. I also knew that Jews were sleeping in the darkness all around me, and I wondered how much longer the two factions could coexist with so much enmity between these conflicting cultures and faiths.

The next day, the research team consisting of Dr. Mike Jiles, professor Chuck Benson, Brigadier General Norm Andersson, West Point Graduate Craig Newmaker, researcher Bonnie Dawson, and literary agent John Nill, all went to the City of David to begin another phase of investigation. Things began to develop at a speed beyond my wildest dreams. In a serendipitous sequence we happened to connect with archaeologist and director of the City of David excavations, Eli Shukron. I mentioned him earlier in chapter one.

Eli Shukron is a rugged looking man with dark eyes and rough calloused hands from twenty years of digging out massive amounts of dirt in and around the City of David and the Gihon Springs. We all were surprised when he unexpectantly agreed to take us on an extensive tour of the underground world of the City of David with its winding system of tunnels. The most exciting part was that this was a behind-the-scenes, no-tourists-allowed, tour.

With headlamps and high hopes we descended into the bowels of the City of David excavation site and down narrow ancient hand-chiseled rock passageways. As tourists kept to the confines of a well-defined and restricted route, we were privy to Eli unlocking gates and chain barricades all along the way. We were first taken to the deep foundation stones of the City of David which were imbedded in the Kidron Valley. I was surprised to see just how far into the ground they were, indicating to me that the Kidron was at the time of David, much deeper, having been filled in with silt over these many years.

Our group was stunned when Eli said, "This is the City of David, but was also the real true location of Zion." He added that Zion had been misplaced in the upper city of Jerusalem and that this was the stronghold of Zion. It was confirming the facts I had gathered, that Zion was in—and could only be right above—the area where we were standing. It also reminded me of the verse in 2 Samuel 5:7: *"Nevertheless David took the stronghold of Zion, (that is, the City of David)."* Again, this verse makes it impossible to dissociate Zion within the City of David—which we have documented Scripturally in this book.

For the research team, 2 Chronicles 3:1 brought it all back to this very spot: *"Now Solomon began to build the house of the Lord at Jerusalem...at the place that David had prepared on the threshing floor of Ornan the Jebusite."*

This was the one and only area of search for the threshing floor as well as the original Zion and the temple location.

THE THRESHING FLOOR—PAST AND FUTURE

Why was the threshing floor so important as the site of the temple? Threshing floors are a flat place for separating wheat from chaff and would have either been cut flat or made flat with paving stones. This was a focal area in the city or village. But, for efficient use, it had to be high enough to gather the wind.

If we look at the Dome of the Rock, it is at an elevated position, yet threshing floors were not located on the top of mountains. People had enough burdens in life without needlessly having to carry large bundles of wheat up a rocky tall slope. They would thresh their wheat at a more accessible locale, where burros or carts could carry the load more easily, yet be high enough to take advantage of the sifting wind. It is easy to anoint the Dome of the Rock as a threshing floor, but the peak is too high for laborers to function at maximum proficiency.

According to the Bible (as referenced above in 2 Chronicles 3:1), the threshing floor is, in effect, the anchor point for the temple. It was in the area of the Gihon Spring and it also seems to be close to where the angel of the Lord stepped in to abort Abraham's attempt to sacrifice his son. The Bible describes how God instructed Abraham to go to the land of Moriah and offer his son as an offering. *"Then Abraham lifted his eyes and looked, and there behind him was a ram caught in a thicket by its horns. So*

Abraham went and took the ram and offered it up for a burnt offering instead of his son" (Genesis 22:13).

Years later, David would buy that same piece of real estate and the temple would be constructed.

Consider this. When Jesus was sacrificed on the cross, His head was crowned with thorns, similar to the thorns of the ensnared ram in the Abraham/Isaac story. Much of the world would reject this Lamb called Jesus, who incidentally died for us just like the ram died as a substitute for Abraham's son. The Bible tells us that judgment awaits *all* those who reject God's Son (our substitute sacrificial ram).

This judgment will occur, I believe, right on the threshing floor where the new temple is built and where Jesus will rule and reign. It will be just like the separating of the wheat (those who are forgiven) and the chaff (those who are not forgiven).

In Matthew 3:12 we read a chilling foretelling of this fact: *"His winnowing fan is in His hand, and He will thoroughly clean out His threshing floor, and gather His wheat into the barn; but He will burn up the chaff with unquenchable fire."*

In this verse, the barn represents heaven—a perfect destination. However, according to Scripture, if you are a person who rejects the Lord, then you are essentially...*toast!*

Eli told us over and over again that this was indeed the stronghold of Zion, and mocked the fact that tradition had located it someplace else for so long. I looked at the huge stones in the dark dampness of the place and thought of Psalm 48:9-13, which says, *"We have thought, O God, on Your lovingkindness, In the midst of Your temple. According to Your name, O God, so is Your praise to the ends of the earth; Your right hand is full of righteousness. Let Mount Zion rejoice, let the daughters of Judah be glad, because of Your judgments. Walk about Zion, and go all around her. Count her towers; mark well her bulwarks; consider her palaces; that you may tell it to the generation following."*

This passage reminded me of the gravity of the moment. I was standing at the base of the stone walls; the same walls that the psalmist spoke of being in the midst of God's temple.

STEPS TO THE POOL

While examining the huge stones from the vantage point of the base at the Kidron Valley, I also was well aware of the fact that I was probably very close to the exact spot where King David had once stood. He was looking up at the Jebusite soldiers who hollered down to him:

> *"You shall not come in here; but the blind and the lame will repel you," thinking, "David cannot come in here." Nevertheless David took the stronghold of Zion (that is, the City of David). Now David said on that day, "Whoever climbs up by way of the water shaft and defeats the Jebusites (the lame and the blind, who are hated by David's soul), he shall be chief and captain."*
>
> *Therefore they say, "The blind and the lame shall not come into the house." Then David dwelt in the stronghold, and called it the City of David. And David built all around from the Millo and inward. So David went on and became great, and the Lord God of hosts was with him* (2 Samuel 5:6-10).

These verses reveal several facts. The walls were so high and the valley so low that the Jebusites actually rebuked David and his amassed army not far from where I was standing. David then sent his men up a water shaft and defeated the Jebusites. I asked Eli, "What water shaft could that be?" He replied that there were many shafts where that could have happened.

The passage also speaks of a *Millo,* and I wondered what that meant. Apparently the Millo was a place of earthen fill because the term comes from the the verb, "to be full."

It was a memorable experience being in the shadow of where I believed the true temple was located, and I was curious as to what else Eli was about to show us.

He then led us into the darkened entry of the long rock-cut channel of Hezekiah's tunnel. One by one, we stepped into the cold, thigh-deep waters flowing from the spring of Gihon. After slogging 30 minutes (approximately 1,750 feet) down the dark and narrow water-flowing channel, we spilled out at the rock peninsula at the southern tip of the City of David.

Eli walked into the squinting glare of a harsh sun, and led the way to the pool of Siloam. He paused and pointed to the stone steps leading to this pool of such biblical fame. He had a connection to this place far beyond what we could ever know. In 2004, he had heard that excavators were about to bring in bulldozers and gouge out dirt for a municipal sewer line. Eli knew the historic significance of the area that was about to be churned up, and wanted to be there if something was uncovered.

The excavation company fired up their equipment and, with black diesel smoke spewing from the exhaust pipe, the big earthmover swung into position. The claw of the bulldozer bit into the weed-sprigged soil. It was then that Eli heard the unmistakable sound of metal scrapping across stone. With arms waving, he frantically shouted for the heavy equipment operator to stop. The man argued back, agitated at the interruption. After all, he had a schedule to keep. But Eli insisted.

The machinery was eventually shut off and Eli dropped to his knees next to the excavator's bucket and brushed away the newly disturbed earth. He then saw it. After sleeping in darkness for many long years, the rocks felt the warm sun upon their faces once again. Eli was looking at the flat surface of ancient descending stone steps. It was a major find which would draw the immediate attention of the world. It was the lost pool of Siloam.

This is the pool where Jesus sent the blind man to wash the mud from his eyes and, after doing so, he could see. The event is written about in John 9:1-11:

> *Now as Jesus passed by, He saw a man who was blind from birth. And His disciples asked Him, saying, "Rabbi, who sinned, this man or his parents, that he was born blind?" Jesus answered, "Neither this man nor his parents sinned, but that the works of God should be revealed in him. I must work the works of Him who sent Me while it is day; the night is coming when no one can work. As long as*

I am in the world, I am the light of the world."

When He had said these things, He spat on the ground and made clay with the saliva; and He anointed the eyes of the blind man with the clay. And He said to him, "Go, wash in the pool of Siloam" (which is translated, Sent). So he went and washed, and came back seeing.

Therefore the neighbors and those who previously had seen that he was blind said, "Is not this he who sat and begged?" Some said, "This is he." Others said, "He is like him." He said, "I am he." Therefore they said to him, "How were your eyes opened?" He answered and said, "A Man called Jesus made clay and anointed my eyes and said to me, 'Go to the pool of Siloam and wash.' So I went and washed, and I received sight."

THE COIN, HEROD, AND THE WESTERN WALL

Eli then took us to the upper section of the drainage/ancient sewer channel that I had been researching in a few months prior. He led us to some stones that had been pried up from the floor which was above the channel and pointed to some flat stone pavers that had long ago been pried up and smashed. I looked down into the darkness of the drainage channel. Eli said, "It was here that the Romans dug up the pavement and entered down from the street. They would kill the hiding Jews who sought refuge during the destruction of the first century revolt."

He paused and spoke more slowly; his words almost seemed to carry along with them a more subdued tone of the tragic events that this place once witnessed. Roman soldiers dropped one by one into an underground channel filled with women and children screaming in unimaginable fear. Men had only a few scant swords to protect themselves and they must have killed a few Roman soldiers, but it did not take long for the Romans to overwhelm them and hack them to death. Everyone was slaughtered, it was the Roman way.

Eli looked at me and said, "I found pots which the people used to store their meager food supplies when hiding down there in the cold and wet. I even uncovered one sword, possibly held by either a soldier or by a defender, but it really does not matter now."

He looked into the opening of the channel below, "Someone probably had dropped the sword and it got lost in the mud for almost two thousand years ago and I found it." He made a shoveling motion for effect, "I was digging, and there it was, all caked in rust and corrosion."

Eli then turned away to walk down the ancient slimy rock-walled drainage ditch that he had dug away so much dirt from. He stopped along the way telling us all about how he excavated year after year in the many tunnels of the City of David. We passed right by the drainage channels coming off the City of David that Nissim had shown me back in July, but I felt it best not to say anything for fear Nissim had told me in confidence. Our guide kept on going up the drainage channel north towards the Temple Mount and he eventually stopped at the underground excavations of the western wall of the Mount.

We were about 30 feet under street level and in the raw illumination of some glaring floodlights. Eli pointed to a long wall of huge stone blocks and said, "Most every scholar believes that the stones that you see here were built by Herod's men. He then spoke from behind a tenuous smile, "I found a coin dated to 20 AD, as I dug beneath a huge stone block down here under the very lowest layer of foundation stones."

The coin was an ancient bronze and that of Valerius Gratus, Prefect under Tiberius15-26 AD. The minting date of the coin as well as its earliest distribution was vintage 20 AD, according to Eli's explanation.

He asked me slowly, "Do you understand what I am saying here?" I paused, surprised at what he had said. "I am telling you that Herod did not build the Western Wall."

I really didn't know how to respond. Here was an eminent archaeologist who had unearthed a long list of world renowned discoveries in the City of David and elsewhere in Jerusalem, and he was now actually telling me that Herod *did not build* the Western Wailing Wall.

My jaw must have dropped, because of what I was hearing. A

famous wall, known the world over, a wall that almost everyone agrees as being the tangible remains of the foundation stones for the biblical temples was not directly built by Herod. The historic implications of what Eli said were monumental.

I did the math, now understanding the enormity of his words. I had read how Herod had suffered from fever, itching, continuous pains in his intestines, tumors of the feet, inflammation in his abdomen, gangrene of the genitals, asthma and foul breath. He died in 4 BC. Now if Eli had dug out a coin from under the lowest layer of stones in the Western Wall which dated to 20 AD, then how could I now, or any scholars for that matter, reconcile the fact that Herod died at least 24 years before the coin somehow made its way under a stone so low in the foundation of the Temple Mount? It was logically as well as practically impossible.

If Eli was telling me a reliable fact, and I have no reason to doubt him, then Herod did not build what he has been so profusely credited with.

After thanking Eli and saying our goodbyes I went into my old cop-mode of research. The dating of walls in Jerusalem began to take on a new light for me, so I decided to go back to other walls located in Jerusalem that may help solve the riddle of the temple location.

CHAPTER 13

SMALL TEMPLE, NEW WALLS

The *New Bible Dictionary* states that Jerusalem was forced to open its gates to the Roman general Pompey in the spring of 63 BC. This was the start of the formal Roman rule in the Holy City. But the general and his troops had a very tough time taking control of the temple.

We know from the Bible that Jewish immigrants returning to Jerusalem from exile in Babylon were allowed to rebuild their temple, but they could not build defense walls for fear of possible Jewish revolt. In time, however, a new temple was eventually started, delayed for a while and then re-started by Zerubbabel and Joshua, son of Jozadak.

Upon completion, it was not impressive compared with the opulent magnificence of that built by Solomon. The Bible describes the disappointment in the appearance of the temple in Ezra 3:12: *"But many of the priests and Levites and heads of the father's house, old men who had seen the first temple, wept with a loud voice when the foundation of this temple was laid before their eyes..."*

Nehemiah returned to Jerusalem in 445 BC, and during his survey at night, (Nehemiah 2:12-55) he saw the beleaguered defense walls of Jerusalem that desperately needed repair. These walls have been suggested as being most notably those that surrounded the temple.

Work went on day and night because of the threatening aggressions of the surrounding enemies. A high wall was needed for protection. Half of the wall builders held weapons while the other half worked tirelessly, trying to repair the defense walls (Nehemiah 4:10-11). After 52 days their task was completed.

In time, other segments of the same walls would be even more fortified during the Hasmonean period. They would prevail until the Romans arrived in 63 BC.[1]

Where was Nehemiah's wall located? Famed archaeologist Kathleen Kenyon believes she found remnants of the Nehemiah and Hasmonean defense walls in Area G, in the City of David above the stepped-stone structure at the top of the slope.[2]

She described them as being sloppily made, but added that the workers were in a bit of a hurry for obvious reasons, and they also used unskilled labor. However, no matter how unattractive, those same walls were stalwart enough to keep the Roman army at bay for three long months. Since these were in the City of David, they are structural relatives of the walls around the stronghold of Zion. It was the temple that was being protected.

We can also be confident that Nehemiah's walls surrounded the original stronghold of Zion in the City of David because it took him only 52 days to complete the immense task. Those fortifications had to be stacked on-top of the original foundation walls that were already there or it would have taken much longer to build.

Even though in disrepair, the original walls were established with foundational stones embedded deep in the soil and the existing exposed stones would allow a new wall to have a distinct edge, resulting in a short completion time.

We can be assured from the Bible that the new temple of Zerubbabel was built within the confines of the original Zion, specifically from what is stated in Jeremiah 30:17-18: *"This is Zion...Behold, I will bring back the captivity of Jacob's tents, and have mercy on his dwelling places; the city shall be built upon its own mound..."*

Again, 2 Samuel 5:7 tells us, *"Nevertheless, David took the stronghold of Zion (that is, the City of David)."* This verse bonds Zion within the City of David, and Joel 3:17 unites the original Zion with the temple *"So shall you know that I am the Lord your*

God, dwelling in Zion My holy mountain." Remember, "My holy mountain" is the place of the temple.

So, it is apparent that the same walls which protected the temple of Zerubbabel in Zion are those that endured until the Romans arrived in Jerusalem.[3]

These defense walls surrounding the temple that met the Romans would have encouraged them, over time, to build an even larger fortress nearby. So the huge Roman military stone citadel, right next to the temple in Zion (City of David), would have to be built out of strategic necessity.

The Romans, because of their pride, could not have a walled defensive position with a revered temple in its close proximity and have an inferior fortress for themselves. So, progressively, a Roman fort to the north was constructed at the present day Dome of the Rock locale. The contentious and rebellious Jews would eventually be living in the shadow of a massive walled Roman fortification looming over them.

THE TIMELINE

Let's quickly review some of the facts that are crucial to the temple location.

We know that the Roman, Pompey, was let into the walled city of Jerusalem, in 63 by Hyrcanus.[4] Keep in mind: this was the walled city and not the walled-in temple confines.

At this time there was no mighty Roman fort on the Temple Mount because the Romans were not in control until after Pompey's siege. It is here that we know Aristobulus rebuffed any surrender and took his men to the temple where they held fast. The only way he could stave off the battle-skilled Romans was because he had the defense wall built on top of the City of David walls by Nehemiah and then fortified by the Hasmoneans.

Years later, according to Josephus, the two complexes coexisted approximately 600 feet apart from connecting colonnades. Josephus further talks in some detail about this closely positioned Roman fort that I believe was in the present day Dome of the Rock 36 acre complex. As Josephus describes, *"...the structure resembled that of a tower, it contained also four other distinct towers at its four corners; whereof the other were but fifty cubits high; whereas that which lay upon the southeast corner was seventy cubits high, that from there the whole temple might be viewed.*[5]

Here we have a perfect description of what one would expect from a larger fortress looking down upon another (subordinate in size) adjacent complex. In fact, in the same chapter from *Jewish War*, Josephus goes on to say. *"...the temple was a fortress that guarded the city (Zion) as was the tower of Antonia a guard to the temple."*

As time continued to elapse, the temple of Herod was completely destroyed during a Jewish revolt. It was burned, dismantled and ripped up to its very footings in 70 AD. Jews were slaughtered wholesale.

Several hundred years later, Muslim control, for the most part, removed Jews from any access to the traditional Temple Mount. After another several centuries people were probably unsure where the temple really had been. The distance of time and Jewish alienation from the land would probably be the reason. However, in searching for the forgotten temple site, they ignored the fact that Jesus said that the temple would be completely gone to the very last stone.

Casting Christ's words carelessly aside, they gazed in awe at what remained of a massive, imposing construct, courtesy of Roman architecture and craft. The abandoned Roman fort was eventually adopted as the temple confines and it was certified by tradition.

So it is today. We have a serious predicament of the world's perception, believing that the Temple Mount is in fact the actual place of Herod's temple, when it is not. The temple built by Herod was to the south, lower in elevation, in Zion, in the City of David, lesser in size than the dominant Roman fort, that in all probability, is an intrusive imposter to the real temple locale.

Yet a quandary exists for traditionalists. This arises in the form of a small bronze coin that was dug out from underneath the huge stone block at the lowest place in the wall. Its position would indicate that Herod, the great builder, might have had no personal involvement in overseeing construction of the wall because he was dead for almost a quarter of a century during the earliest phase of that section of wall being built.

Had the coin fallen from the pocket of a worker? Had a Roman soldier carelessly let it slip from his grasp? No one will ever know, but the historical implications need to be addressed.

If Herod did not personally oversee the building of the wall as Eli told me, then who did?

In the date of 20 AD, Tiberius Caesar would have been the Roman ruler—and the man whose coin which was made in his honor, and found two thousand years later by Eli, was Valerius Gratus, the Prefect Under Tiberius. However, it is not being inferred here that Herod did not have any involvement in working on the Roman Fort Antonia. It is clear from Josephus that he did. But the huge wall that credits his name with such certainty, may actually be a missplaced pronouncement of notoriety.

It's interesting that Tiberius is believed by scholars as the face on the coin when Jesus said, *"Render therefore to Caesar the things that are Caesar's, and to God the things that are God's"* (Matthew 22:21). I also think we should not render to Herod what he did *not* build—the wall—and what he really *did* build, a temple in the city of David.

OLD SYNAGOGUES

The next day, our team went to the oldest synagogue in Jerusalem. According to *Karaite* tradition the original synagogue called *Tifereth* was built about 1,300 years ago. The building was damaged in the 1948 War of Independence and the Six Day War in 1967. It had been renovated with modern trappings inside, but the original arched support pillars still stood. The archways pointed in the direction the original synagogue once faced.

Taking compass readings of the building, Dr. Michael Jiles, who was with us, went outside and climbed a rickety wooden ladder leaning on the side of the building and leading to the roof. Once on top, he took his compass and looked over to the Temple Mount. Dr. Jiles hollered down to the waiting team and said the compass points south of the Temple Mount in the general direction of the Ophal, in the environs of the City of David, and not directly at the Dome of the Rock as would be expected—if that was indeed the real temple location.

The significance to all this was the fact that ancient synagogues in Jerusalem apparently all pointed to the place of Solomon's temple. According to Dr. Lee Levine, professor of history and archaeology at the Hebrew University of Jerusalem, *"Archaeological evidence reveals that beginning in the third and fourth centuries almost all synagogues were oriented toward Jerusalem. The orientation was sometimes expressed by an elaborate exterior façade, and always by the building's interior design: the focal wall would face Jerusalem...Those standing in Jerusalem shall direct their hearts toward the Temple."*[6]

I had spoken with many other scholars on the matter of the ancient synagogues in Jerusalem facing the temple and they all relayed that the temple location was not only prayed directly toward, but it was also logical that synagogues all over Israel, as well as in Jerusalem, did indeed face the temple as well.

As I mentioned earlier, the Pilgrim of Bordeaux arrived at the Church of the Holy Sepulcher in 333 AD (which was still under construction), and wrote down his observations. He recorded that while looking east from the Church of the Holy Sepulcher he saw stone walls with foundations going down to the Tyropoean Valley.

The pilgrim was looking due east and was staring directly at the traditional Temple Mount area. He said absolutely nothing about it being the temple site, but rather he describes the stone walls (all of the stone walls) that he was looking at as the praetorium of the Romans. These walls would have survived the Roman/Jewish war of 66-70 AD and were the property of the fort itself. The praetorium was there in all its glory, according to the Bordeaux Pilgrim, which he wrote was the place where Jesus was sentenced to death.

I wanted to see for myself the same view that the Bordeaux Pilgrim saw from the periphery area of the Church of the Holy Sepulcher. Because of obvious security concerns I was not allowed on the roof of the church, but adjacent is the Lutheran Church of the Redeemer. Artist Chuck Benson and I climbed the 223 narrow, winding stone steps, and from the lofty tower we both looked east just as the Bordeaux Pilgrim had in the fourth century.

There it was! The whole landscape was swallowed up with the view of the Temple Mount. The pilgrim had to have been seeing the walls of the Roman fort. I knew then and there that, at least according to the Bordeaux Pilgrim, the Temple Mount we see today was indeed the former fort of the Roman Tenth Legion.

Next to me stood Chuck, who was drawing away on his sketch pad at the vistas where we were looking. With a ripening smile, he turned to me and said, "It looks like all the facts in your theory are really adding up!"

THE MUSEUM CLUE

On a Sabbath (Saturday), our November 2013 team was quite delighted that the Israeli Museum in Jerusalem was open—when almost everything else was closed. So we took advantage of the time off from our hectic schedule to enjoy the amazing museum and its incredible exhibits.

As I walked past one ancient monument and statue after another, my eyes settled upon a broken stone plaque mounted on a wall in the Herod exhibit area. It was not that big, but it was inscribed with the following metal etched signage:

THIS GREEK INSCRIPTION, DISCOVERED IN EXCAVATIONS SOUTH OF THE TEMPLE MOUNT RECORDS THE CONSTRUCTION OF A PAVEMENT PAID FOR WITH A DONATION BY A MAN FROM RHODES. IT IS POSSIBLE THAT THE PAVEMENT WAS A COSTLY *OPUS SECTILE* FLOOR, IN KEEPING WITH JOSEPHUS' DESCRIPTION: THE OPEN COURT WAS FROM END TO END VARIEGATED WITH PAVING OF ALL MANNER OF STONES (JEWISH WARS 5, 192).

An *Opus Sectile* as mentioned above is an ancient Roman method of cutting stones and inlaying them in opulent floors to make a beautiful design. It is probable from this inscription on the stone that it was a memorial marker for a donor to the temple. It seems that even old Herod the Great had ways of fundraising and then offering recognition (brick *Opus Sectile*) as a token for their donations. But the most interesting fact about the stone mounted on the wall of the museum was that it was found south of the Temple Mount which only could be either on the *Ophal* or in the *City of David*. In any event, it is right where we were all now believing that the true temple area should be.

Another factor relating to the stone is that it was an *Opus Sectile* which was in the open court (temple?) area. It was not a lightning bolt from heaven for our theory, but a brick in the wall of our thesis which came from the temple open court itself.

WAS SOMETHING MISSING?

Time was running short on this final trip before I put this book to rest. I had the feeling that there was something I was missing—some piece of the puzzle that was right in front of me, but I was not finding. It is often the most obvious that slips past, even with the most ardent scrutiny. But was it really missing, or was it something I was about to see?

We called Eli Shukron on his cell phone for one more pass at our questioning, even though I was sure his traditional views would never transfer his beliefs from the Temple Mount as the location of the true temples. I had so little time with him to make my case when we had last met, and besides I certainly didn't want to insult what he seemed to hold so firmly.

This book started when I met Eli and now, after so many pages of research, it will come full circle to a wondrous moment.

When Eli had first shown me the underground world of the City of David only days earlier, I had not expected to see anything more amazing than we had already witnessed. It was certainly a red letter day, but isn't it true of life that just when you think nothing could get any better, God reaches down and you are handed something beyond gold.

After meeting Eli this time in the City of David, he surprised me by taking us to an underground sanctuary. He told me that just a few individuals had ever been allowed there. I had the feeling of this being a nexus moment in my research, not to mention my entire life.

So, when he led us to an underground limestone group of rooms and chambers, I felt the deep assurance in my soul that I was at a location of holy construct.

He had found this place about two years earlier, and since then workers have painstakingly been sifting dirt and hauling it away. Eli said, "This is a worship area, We do not know exactly what it is, but it is from the first temple period and possibly even before." Then waving his hand in a sweeping motion, he told us, "This is the only worship area in the City of David. Everything is perfect."

Eli then pointed to a carved-out hole in the stone floor and said, "This is an olive press to make oil."

My heart and mind raced. Leviticus 21:12 tells us: "*...nor shall he go out of the sanctuary, nor profane the sanctuary of his God: for the consecration of the anointing oil of his God is upon him.*"

Once the oil was sprinkled on the priest, he was forbidden to leave the sanctuary. This sacred place was at ground zero—right where I thought the temple to be. So, logically, one might assume that if the priest had the anointing oil present, this well may be the actual temple location.

Eli then walked over and bent down, pointing to a hand-cut straight channel running the full length of the room. He stood and said matter-of-fact, even though a sledge hammer would have had as much subtlety to my brain, "This is a channel for blood and, as you can see, this room is raised. It is here there was an altar for sacrificing small animals, such as sheep." His extended hand showed us the path of draining blood, and he explained, "The blood went into the floor over there and the animals were tied up here."

He then stepped over to a corner in the stone wall and his fingers poked through to a hole in the edge of the stone. He told us, "This is where a ring was set to tie up the animal being slaughtered. Eli smiled, as proud as if he had made the sanctuary himself. "Everything is perfect; few people have been in here to see it."

Eli continued, "I knew that something happened here I did not know what? When I started to clean it (take away the dirt) I began to understand. This is the place of something huge and we are in the heart of it. This is an area of worship and praying and a place where people connected with God. And from that we understand what happened here in the time of the first temple period and even before."

Images of first temple period underground worship area that is close to the Gihon spring that the author believes may be part of Solomon's temple. Photo courtesy of Eli Shukron.

SO AMAZING!

Team member Bonnie Dawson, who had put so much time and effort into this project, was so moved by what she was hearing that her eyes were cupped with tears. After Eli reiterated several times that we were in the City of David, in Zion, in the very place of blood sacrifices, in a location that made anointing oil that was put on the priests and the animals being sacrificed and that it all was right at the Gihon Spring, Bonnie just could not contain her exuberance and almost jumped in Eli's arms.

It was a burst of uncharacteristic emotion for the usually staid Bonnie, when she stepped over and gave Eli a kiss on his cheek, exclaiming, "This is all so amazing, so very amazing."

Bonnie rubbed a knuckle over her eyes and cheeks, wiping away tears of joy brought on by the moment's gravity. We all, including Bonnie and Eli, had a good laugh as Bonnie blushed with embarrassment. Eli, however, seemed to blush more.

The moment brought us back to the realization that we are all human, possibly stepping on the very stones that the sandals of priest and prophets had worn smooth.

Just then, climbing up out of the shaft area was my friend Nissim. With his big smile, stocky frame, and wild, long grey beard, he looked like Santa Claus climbing out of the chimney with dust and dirt all over him. He had been digging all day and heard I was in the area and wanted to say hello.

We all paused to greet him, and then Eli continued, "This is the place of worship and sacrifice."

Nissim interrupted, almost mischievous in mannerism, and then added, "I found animal bones all over the palace. There were lots of bones from the sacrifices."

Again, I looked at our surroundings. Here was a beautiful hand stone-cut room with two adjoining rooms where anointing oil was made, and where we knew sacrifices had been performed. The whole amazing moment was right out of the manual for what one might expect for the procedures in the temple confines—and it was all smack-dab in the middle of the City of David as well as the biblical stronghold of Zion.

I asked Eli, "How close are we to the Gihon Spring?" He answered, "About ten meters (30 feet). You have everything together here close to the spring, close to the water, living water —and we know that a place of worship to God is near to water." He paused, "This is the foundation of the earth that connects with God."

As he continued to show our team around, Eli pointed out two small recessed areas about the size of a low ceiling walk-in closet. One of the spaces was empty but the other had an upright stone approximately the size of a cemetery headstone. There was no writing on it, which was typical for ancient Jews. Eli explained that the fact it was still standing upright after all these years was a sign that somebody long ago considered this to be an extremely sacred place.

It was at that moment that the confluence of intellect and emotion collided. I knew where I was—somewhere in the complex of Solomon's temple. Exactly where I did not know. But Eli had said that there were many other areas that needed excavating, and I assumed that treasures of historic significance were only a few feet away from where I was standing.

More excavations will follow and I wondered what the dirt was silently holding in its concealing embrace.

We were in the City of David, the site of the temple. How could we doubt the significance of this special place? It was right in the well-defined precincts of the stronghold of Zion. The nearby flowing Gihon Spring closed the target to a much more defined area. This had to be very near to the threshing floor that David had bought from the Jebusite. This was, is, and shall forever be ground zero of the temple placement.

SUNKEN GATES

What could possibly remain of Herod's temple? Really nothing, because Christ had said that it would be obliterated to the very last stone. The uprooted stones were carried off for other construction projects and the temple area was bare—with a lonely farmer's field as the only memorial.

As Josephus had recorded, nothing remained of Herod's temple. It was so savagely devastated that no one could even tell that anything had been there at all. But that was not true of what remained of Solomon's temple, which could have been lower, covered over by the debris and fill during the Babylonian destruction.

The Book of Lamentations is a reflection of what many believe was written by the prophet Jeremiah describing in vivid narrative the ravaging of Jerusalem and Solomon's temple in 587 BC, which was the beginning of the Babylonian exile. In Lamentations 2:7-9, we read: *"...The Lord has spurned His altar, He has abandoned His sanctuary...The Lord has purposed to destroy the wall of the daughter of Zion...her gates have sunk in the ground..."*

These verses point out that Solomon's temple is clearly at Zion and that its wreckage was *beyond* annihilation. It even says that the gates *have sunk in the ground.* So when Herod's construction crews arrived, they needed to fill in whatever was remaining from any former temple destruction. If this truly was the temple location then it certainly would have been Roman engineers working for Herod on this site, which probably used mostly local Jewish labor. But, in any event, the temple of Solomon would need to be covered over flat to be able to build a successive temple by Herod upon any remaining rubble.

The room I now was in with Eli had many vertical support beams to keep the fill dirt overhead from crashing down. It may have been dirt deposited at the time of Solomon's temple being destroyed and/or renovated to allow the grading requirements of construction.

One very odd, unexplainable feature that I saw in the sanctuary area was the existence of V cuts in the stone floor. There were three "V's carved about two inches deep and twenty inches long in the stone below our feet. Eli was also curious as to what they were.

In thinking it over, I suggested they may be slots that stabilized the legs of the slaughter tables. More than likely, the animals being sacrificed did not enjoy being held down with a man standing over them holding a knife to their throats. Another explanation might be that they were there to stabilize a laver-type basin, which was filled with water.

I felt we might have overstayed our welcome. Perhaps Eli was pushing the bounds of protocol, so when he appeared a tad anxious, I suggested we leave. Eli had probably shown more cards than he had intended, but I am so very grateful to him for pulling back the curtain on such an amazing find.

I believe I may have stood on holy ground:

- A place that ran with the blood of countless sacrifices to the Lord.
- A place that ran with the clear water of the Gihon Spring.
- A place that ran with the anointing oils from olives that were crushed in a press on that floor.

Then there were the angled holes in the corner of the wall where I inserted my own fingers that once held the rings which tied struggling animals just before they were sacrificed as sin offerings.

I knew from reading Josephus (*Antiquities*, V3, 8.6) that even as far back as Moses and the tabernacle, in the procedures enacted, spring water was essential in purification of priests. Josephus writes, *"Moses had sprinkled Aaron's vestments, himself, and his sons, with the blood of the beasts that were killed, and had purified them with spring water and ointment, they became God's priests."*

Spring water (moving pure water) and ointments (pressed olive oil) were absolute essentials needed to purify. The only running water available to Moses was that from the split rock and the only spring water available in Jerusalem at the temple was the Gihon Spring, in the City of David, in the stronghold of Zion. Then, right in front of me was the olive press, chiseled so smooth and round in the stone floor. And if all that was not off-the-chart amazing, I remembered that right above us, probably only feet away, archaeologists had found burnt clay *bulla* stamps which reveal the name *Gemariah*, the scribe who is mentioned in the Bible and who had his chamber in the upper court of the House of the Lord (Jeremiah 36:10). It was enough to take one's breath away.

SCRIPTURE HOLDS THE ANSWER

As I turned to go, Eli said, "Bob wait a moment."

I stopped as he commented with a bemused expression. *"I know you believe that the temple was at the Gihon. I have to tell you that I am not able to say that for obvious reasons because of who I am and what I have written over the years. But I must say that the temple absolutely had to have spring water and there is no spring on the traditional Temple Mount. It says in Numbers that the ritual of purification of the red cow* (red heifer) *had to have running pure spring water."* (See Numbers 19).

He looked down the aforementioned mysterious shaft and said so softly that I barely could hear him, *"And the Gihon is the only place that has running water from a spring."* I didn't utter a word, other than to smile at his much appreciated comments.

As we left the tunnel to meet my awaiting friends and step once again into the full yawn of the Kidron Valley, I had to pause for a moment. I looked at my research team who stood silent, waiting for me to join them.

Craig Newmaker commented, "I think we all feel the same about what we just experienced." Craig's voice was somber, but he was always calm and sure with whatever he said. He was, after all, a West Point graduate and a former Army Ranger. He looked at me with a locked-on gaze and added, "There's not one shred of doubt that what we just saw and where we just stood is the place of Solomon's temple."

Had we indeed just brushed past holy remains? Had we just stood over the same olive press that had crushed olives which produced the oil that had anointed King Solomon himself when he rode a mule to the gurgling purification waters of the Gihon to be crowned king?

A BOY AND A FATHER

Recently, while walking past the Wailing Wall at the traditional Temple Mount, I saw a father holding the Torah and reading it to his boy, who was sitting on his lap. I believe that Jesus was read to by His father in a similar way.

The stones of the wall mirrored in this boy's eyes from an alabaster reflection of a low-arching summer sun. The boy nestled in his father's arms reminded me that cherished beliefs are so important to our emotional balance. If someone comes along and disrupts the equilibrium of that belief, it may be very uncomfortable and almost frightening. But, just maybe, that boy will one day read from the sacred text in 2 Samuel 5:3-9 and come to realize that the City of David and a place called Zion (*Metsudat Tsion*), are one-in-the-same. He would learn that long ago, God directed a king named David to buy a threshing floor there as a special place to build God's temple; and that the ark was then placed inside that temple; and under the ground, in the bowels of the earth, a spring that brought water to the temple still runs as a consecrated reminder of truth: *"A fountain shall flow from the house of the Lord"* (Joel 3:18).

I wanted so much to show the young boy a photograph I held in my hand that I had just found displayed in a window in the old city of Jerusalem and had bought. But I would never dream of disrupting a tender moment between father and son worshiping at a place they held so sacred.

The black and white photo was taken in 1936 from an airplane and it showed the area south of the Temple Mount, more specifically the City of David, the place I had come to know well as the Gihon Spring. I had read a prophetic verse in the Bible from Micah 3:12: *"Zion shall be plowed like a field, Jerusalem shall become heaps of ruins, and the mountains of the temple like the bare hills of the forest."*

The 1936 photo vividly showed the view over the Gihon as freshly plowed fields in a descending series of terraced farmland. This area of Zion was plowed under exactly as predicted in the eighth century BC. Conversely, the Dome of the Rock has not now, nor has ever been plowed—nor has the Temple Mount walled enclosure been uprooted and removed as Christ prophesied.

The photo now hangs in my office as a daily reminder that we should follow the directives of Scripture and never be deflected in our search for truth by any traditions, no matter how popular or mutually confirmed by others.

SINCERE, MISTAKEN ACCEPTANCE

I have found that in any search involving biblical narratives, man-crafted traditions have a very subtle way of straying us far away from scriptural directives. Long ago, traditions started seeping ever so slowly down into the foundations of the church and, in time, silently established deep roots that became unnoticed tethers of church doctrine. Over enough centuries, some traditions have become so entrenched that if anyone even dares to challenge the church's controlling interest, they are then summarily chastised, punished, or even banished from the faith.

In the Middle Ages, when thousands of reformers dared defy views on the interpretation of ecclesiastically accepted Scripture interpretation of the time, the offenders were castigated. Many were lashed to a post as straw bundles were placed at their feet. The crowds that gathered would often jeer as well as cheer when the torch's flame touched the parched pyre, igniting it into a raging inferno. The condemned frantically yanked on the sooty chains and pleaded—between ebbing screams—which soon faded into empty silence. The message sent out to the masses by church leaders was..."*Do not ever challenge our traditional views any time, or over any place.*"

Jesus knew how man's traditions could cloud His divine message, so the apostles wrote it all down for us in order that we would not have any subsequent confusion. Christ quoted from Scripture often and never relied on oral interpretations or alterations of the sacred Word from anyone.

Traditions are mentioned in the New Testament fourteen times, all of which are framed in a negative and derogatory light, except on a few occasions specifying a demanded imperative for strict adherence to what Scripture presented in the past, His words, and those of the apostles. Man-made addenda to Scripture are strictly forbidden by Christ, which include non-biblically based beliefs passed off as divinely prescribed.

The Western Wailing Wall in Jerusalem is, of course, viewed as a tangible connection to a perceived past location. The object thus becomes a surrogate manifestation of a place to worship and, over time, it has morphed into a holy object itself. It becomes uncontested as sacred today as if it had been confirmed holy long ago by divine, legitimate fiat.

When the temple of Herod was destroyed, a vacuum of worshipful adoration was created. The physical place was gone so a suitable replacement was sought and conveniently found by travelers to Jerusalem around the turn of the first millennium. They saw a huge high walled fortress and summarily adopted it as a holy relic. No one can doubt the sincerity of people who accept it as such today. We all want the comfort of being where miracles and wonders made their stamp on planet earth.

This is no blemish on Jews who bow and pray daily at the Western Wailing Wall. I have stood for hours and watched them reverently place written requests in the rock crevices and pray hour upon hour, believing it to be truly a holy place. And since I am an imperfect man trying to find truth in an imperfect world, maybe it is I who has erred in my opinions. But, when I use the perfect source of the Bible, and it is telling me over and over again that the temple has to be in the City of David, and that it has to be in the stronghold of Zion, then astute and committed attention needs to be adhered too and the distracting pull of traditions inherently ignored.

1936 aerial photo of the traditional Temple Mount

platform/Dome of the Rock. Note the plowed terraced farm fields where the City of David is located. Micah 3:12 says, *"Zion shall be plowed like a field. Jerusalem shall become heaps of ruins, And the mountains of the temple like the bare hills of the forest..."* (Micah 3:12).

The 12-acre Jebusite walled-in fortress around the time of David's conquest. It would include the places known as the Threshing Floor of Ornan, the Stronghold of Zion, the Gihon Spring, and the City of David. It is also the location described in Scripture as the place of the true temple locations.

The temple of Solomon in the City of David. (Note the rocky protrusion above where the Roman Fort Antonia will be built several hundreds years later.)

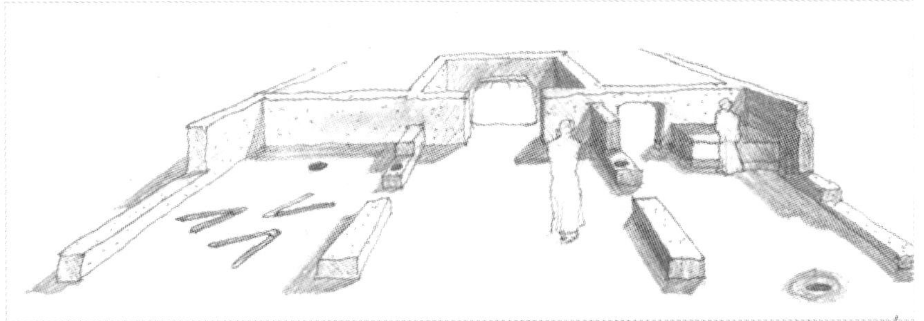

The underground sanctuary Eli showed our team.

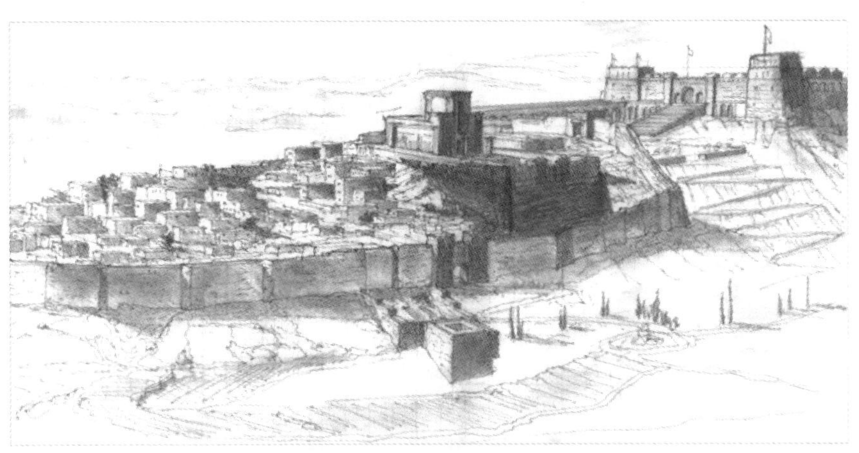

Herod's temple with Roman Fort Antonia above.

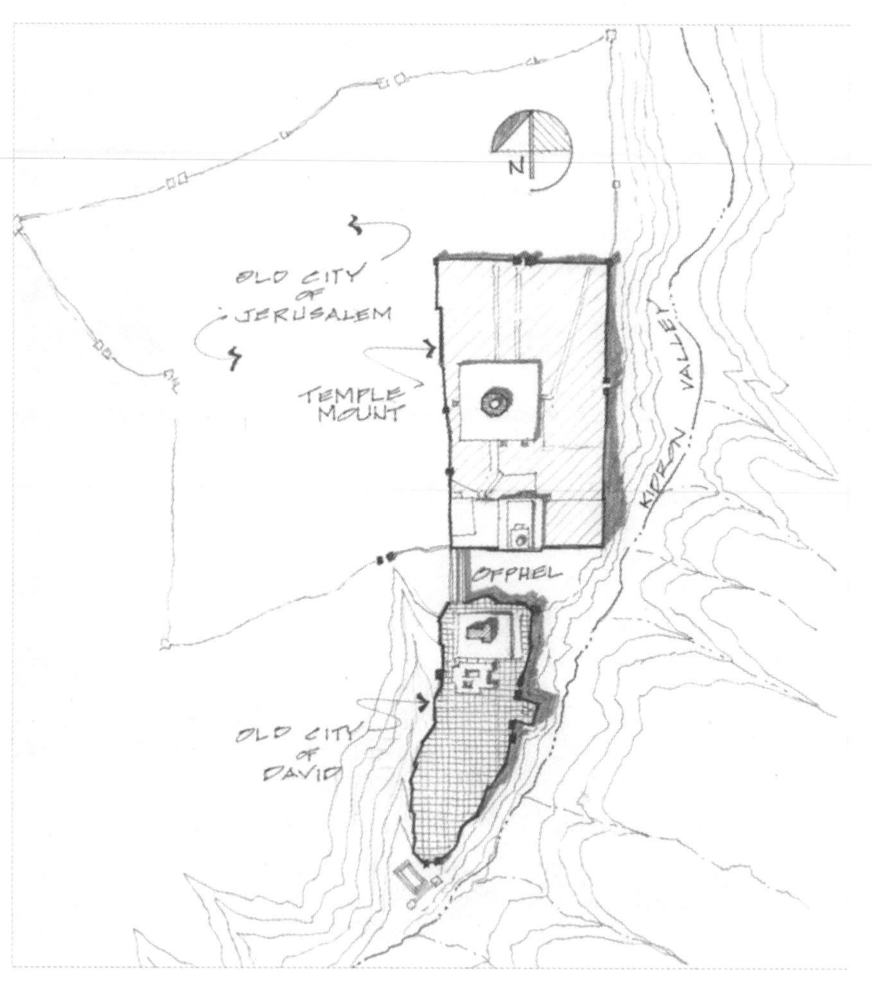

A blend of modern and ancient. The modern traditional Temple Mount with the Muslim Dome of the Rock to the north, and the old City of David with Herod's temple to the south. Note the twin 600-foot connecting bridges that Josephus described.

This is the sketch that architect Chuck Benson drew while in a tall church tower next to the Church of the Holy Sepulcher. It is a depiction of what the Bordeaux Pilgrim would have seen in 333 AD when he described looking due east from this very location and recorded that he saw the long wall of the Roman fort, which described the praetorium where Pilate heard the case against Christ. As seen in this sketch, there is no way that what the Pilgrim described is in any way the temple area (which is a quarter-mile south in the City of David).

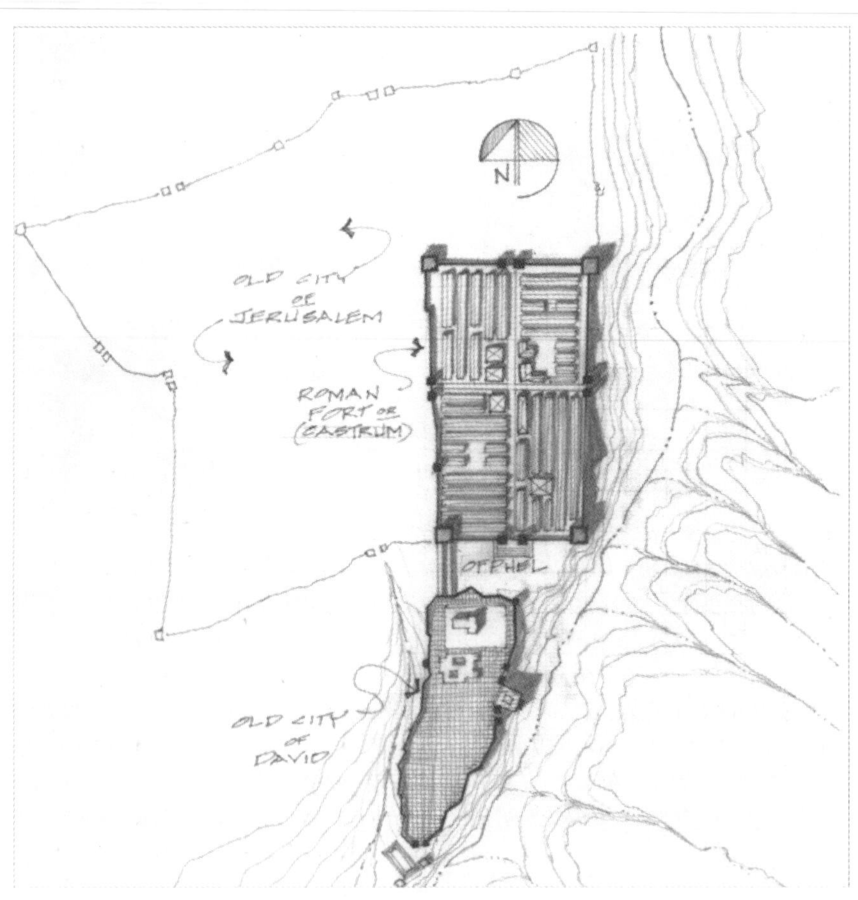

Overhead sketch with Roman Fort Antonia to the north (modern location of the Temple Mount) and the City of David to the south with temple.

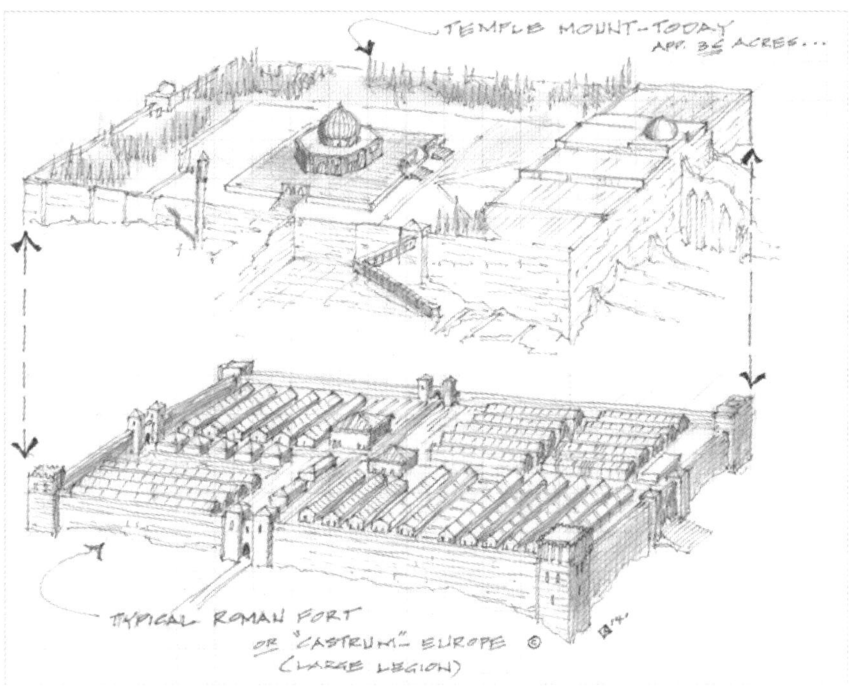

The Temple Mount today as it overlays above the Roman Fort Antonia at the time of Christ.

Illustrations by Chuck Benson.

Part II

The Future Temples

CHAPTER 14

TEMPLE OF THE GREAT TRIBULATION

Two thousand years ago, Jesus walked out of the Judean hills and claimed to be the Son of God. However, tradition was so entrenched that no matter what He did or said, many would not believe. To some He would be called the Christ, but to most He would be considered a fraud—even though He performed many miracles and fulfilled every ancient Jewish prophecy regarding the promised Messiah.

The Bible predicts the events surrounding the time of Christ's reappearance to earth, and according to ancient Scripture, He will definitely appear. And based on current happenings, this time seems imminent. But certain world events need to take place prior to this moment. In the Bible, Paul the Apostle gives us these alerts: *"That Day will not come unless the falling away comes first, and the man of sin is revealed, the son of perdition, who...sits as God in the temple of God, showing himself that he is God"* (2 Thessalonians 2:3-4).

These verses speak of two signs. One is a falling away of the church (apostasy) which is a demonstrable departure from the faith. We see this trend today as marriage rates are dwindling and cohabitation is rising; biblical mandates on sexual behavior are radically ignored or modified, and social morals that were once considered egregiously taboo are culturally adopted. The cancer of today's apostasy is a malignancy that slowly eats away at the heart of the church, the soul of the church, and eventually the *mind* of the church.

THE MAN OF SIN

The second thing that needs to happen is for the man of sin (antichrist) to be revealed.

The arrival of the antichrist to the world's stage has been anticipated since the times of the earliest Church fathers. We are all still waiting. The Jews had been prolifically ousted from their land as far back as the Romans and more comprehensively during the time of the seventh century by the Muslims. So, with that in mind, an interesting clue emerges from the pages of the Bible that brings the antichrist's arrival to a more contemporary time-frame.

Jesus said, *"Therefore when you see the 'abomination of desolation,' spoken of by Daniel the prophet, standing in the holy place" (whoever reads, let him understand), then let those who are in Judea flee to the mountains. Let him who is on the housetop not go down to take anything out of his house. And let him who is in the field not go back to get his clothes. But woe to those who are pregnant and to those who are nursing babies in those days! And pray that your flight may not be in winter or on the Sabbath"* (Matthew 24:15-20).

This verse seems to reveal that the antichrist will come only after Jews are in the land and under Jewish law... *"And pray that your flight may not be in winter or on the Sabbath."* For far more than a millennia, Israel has not been in control of their land...that is, until around the 1947 time frame. So fleeing on the Sabbath, it seems, would not apply to an earlier date when Jews were absent from the land and without legal control. But it certainly would apply today because the Jewish people are legally in possession of Israel and practicing Torah directives.

This antichrist may be alive right now and is planning evil intent from unknown shadows. A conjectured outline of his personage that is based upon biblical characteristics reveals a man who will be very charismatic. He will be someone who has learned how to use the system from history's roll call of masterful deceivers. The gullible masses will be awed and swayed by him and will become malleable and willing conscripts. Peace offered at any price by the antichrist will be the opiate that will dull perceptive minds and propel him on in his power grab. This man will say "tolerance and peace is here,"and the masses will swallow his schemes hook-line-and-sinker.

Scripture tells us, " *"Through his cunning he shall cause deceit to prosper under his rule; and he shall exalt himself in his heart. He shall destroy many...he shall come in peaceably and seize the kingdom by intrigue."* (Daniel 8:25; 11:21).

This evil individual will have a strong and imposing look. His slick words will be eloquent, varnished, and convincing. They will be silky, sinful words spawned of Satan. This man will endure some kind of head injury and survive it (Revelation 13:3). His seemingly miraculous recovery will make him appear to be all the more god-like. He will gather support from unbelievers because, after all, he is the ultimate unbeliever.

The apostate churches may be none-the-wiser by that point and will cast aside traditional beliefs and church affiliations. A one-world religion based upon humanism and satanic precepts will preempt long held world faith structures. Society will be so jaundiced in their faith, and become so anti-Bible that just mentioning the word Jesus could result in condemnation from those who once held that name so dear.

At first, the antichrist will have the stealth of a bird, silently gliding in front of a blinding sun, but then he will be unabashedly blunt when enormous power is finally in his grasp. The Bible says that even the very elect will be deceived by this man (Matthew 24:24). But not all believers will buy his schemes and some will even die resisting his cause.

Many say that the church will need to be raptured first for any of this to happen, thus creating a spiritual vacuum that the antichrist can more easily fill. But whether the rapture is pre-tribulation, during, or after, it will be God's plan that will unfold for His glory and for His purpose.

However, being a follower of Christ will drastically affect directional happenings in both this world and beyond. Disavowing Christ and entering an alliance with the antichrist (such as taking the infamous sign of 666 upon hand or forehead) will have ominous eternal consequences.

THE THIRD TEMPLE

Somewhere in his rise to the summit of power, the antichrist will make it possible for the Jews to rebuild their temple. It would take a person of great influence to convince the Muslims to allow the building of a temple—which most likely would be somewhere on the Temple Mount.

Almost every scholar believes without question that the Temple Mount is the place of the first and second temples, so it goes without saying that once a deal is brokered by the antichrist, that the third temple will be constructed—and it seems most probable that it will be built on the Temple Mount platform. This will add to the antichrist's astonishing perception as being a miracle-worker. The age-old feud will appear to be at long last neutralized.

The third temple could also be constructed in the manner of a tabernacle (tent) as the Hebrews had in the desert wanderings, but no matter what its configuration may be, it will be looked upon as the temple of God.

After almost 2,000 years, a new temple will become a reality and rise upon the landscape of Jerusalem once again. Some will look at the antichrist and call him a mastermind for arranging the building of the temple, yet others will begin to call him "Messiah."

The Jews will wildly cheer when the temple is finished and immediately commence temple functions, as well as ancient blood sacrifices. The Jews will be delirious with joy, singing and dancing with shouts of *l'chaim*, but then after three and a half years, the antichrist will demand that the blood sacrifices be stopped in the temple. He will then do the unthinkable and enter the temple and declare himself to be God.

When the antichrist makes this declaration, the Bible calls this event the "abomination of desolation," and it will forever be known as the greatest sacrilege in all the pages of human history. The mask of peace that was enjoyed for a time will be ripped off and the evil face of violent tribulation will be exposed. The world will pivot to brutal savagery and vile religious persecution for three-and-a-half horrendous years.

The deceived world will come to fiercely despise, condemn, and want to take control of Israel. When that happens, the stage will be set for a final climax which will eclipse all the worst the world's wars have ever known. Those future cries, if they could be heard today, would cause the bravest of souls to wither in whimpering fear. The sad truth is that people will bring to fruition this terrible Armageddon themselves, because they turned their back on the very God who gave them the breath of life.

Israel team member Norm Andersson, a retired Brigadier General, described what may happen during the tribulation period in stark terms. He believes we are living in uniquely ominous times that cast a rapidly darkening shadow upon humanity's precariously approaching horizon. And poised to take advantage of it all, the antichrist awaits his moment of horrific opportunity to deceive and decimate.

He said that by worshiping as well as uniting with the false antichrist, then God almighty will exert His righteous judgment upon them. It will seem as if all the artillery of heaven and hell is unleashed. The judgment will be so unspeakable that God will have to step in to halt the total eradication of all mankind. General Norm relayed to me that in Matthew 24:22 it warns: *"...unless those days were shortened, no flesh would be saved; but for the elect's sake those days will be shortened."* We also talked about what is written in Revelation 9, and he reminded me about verse 15 which says that on a certain day during the tribulations, a third of the world's population will die.

I could not help but think about the mind-stunning biblical prediction that two billion people in a 24-hour period will be part of mass eradication. At no other point in history could that even be possible! But now in our modern times, too many countries have devastating nuclear capabilities that could end life as we know it.

Man's final destiny, however, is not at the whim of mad men with fingers on buttons that send missiles and bombs carrying payloads enough to herald total annihilation. Man has control of his own eternal destiny, but only if he accepts and follows the

Almighty. God always warns all whom reject Him. He cautions about this devious intruder who we call the antichrist and the calamity he will bring upon the world at the end of the age.

We have been clearly alerted, for it has been foretold in the Bible—then, and now. But many will be unaware of their impending doom. It will be just as it was in the days of Noah. The flood was imminent and the people were warned, yet did nothing. Today, the antichrist is coming, and the world has been warned, yet most will do absolutely nothing.

CHRIST'S RULE AND REIGN

So how does the temple's location intersect with all of this? The third temple is a domino ready to fall, commencing an eminent world disaster of indescribable proportions. But, as detailed above, God has a plan and that includes Christ's return. After a time period of three-and-a-half years of world conflict, He descends with the saints and will gather the nations together for one final swift and decisive battle. All earthly kingdoms will be utterly annihilated. All who rejected Christ and unite with the antichrist will drop where they stand at the sound of the Lord's voice. The birds of the air will gorge on the heaping mounds of decaying flesh. The mental image of millions of birds pecking away at decomposing flesh that bears the *666 mark of the antichrist* sends a chill down my spine. It will, however, be the end of the age and the beginning anew with Christ ruling and reigning for a thousand years.

Scripture does not give us the disposition of the Tribulation temple (the third) where the antichrist declares himself to be God, but it is safe to assume that it is either completely abandoned or more likely destroyed from the apocalyptic war or by cataclysmic, tectonic events that are mentioned in the Bible.

THE FOURTH TEMPLE

God's Word, however, speaks of yet another temple (the fourth) that will appear on the Israeli landscape after Christ's triumphant return in glory.

This fourth temple is where Christ will rule and reign during the Millennial kingdom and will hereafter be referred to in this book as the Millennial temple. The precise details concerning this temple (Ezekiel 40:1-47:1) are difficult to explain and have led to an assortment of interpretations. Aside from interpretive nuances and eschatology assumptions, it is safe to say that the Millennial temple will be as literal as other preceding temples.

This Millennial temple will be built relatively close in time after the Tribulation temple but will be much different than all previous ones. In fact, according to the Bible, it will be vastly larger in size and scope, with the temple courts being approximately one mile square.[1]

In spite of its bigger dimensions, however, it will be placed in the same Gihon precinct where Solomon's, Zerubbabel's and Herod's temples rested. These three passages are significant:

- 1 Kings 9:3: *"I have consecrated this house which you have built to put My name there forever..."*
- Zechariah 6:12-15: *"Behold the Man whose name is the Branch! From His place He shall branch out, and He shall build the temple of the Lord...He shall bear the glory, and shall sit and rule on His throne...Even those from afar shall come and build the temple of the Lord..."*
- Zechariah 8:2-3: *"'I am zealous for Zion with great zeal. With great fervor, I am zealous for her.' Thus says the Lord: 'I will return to Zion, and dwell in the midst of Jerusalem. Jerusalem will be called the City of Truth. The Mountain of the Lord of hosts, the Holy Mountain.'"*

The Bible literally shouts across the ages, that it is compulsory for the Millennial temple to be built in Zion, in the City of David at the Gihon.

The Branch in Zechariah 6 is obviously King Messiah and Zion is the designation of the City of David, which is the area of the Gihon Spring. Again, the words "Holy Mountain" is the actual place of the temple in Zion. So, it is King Messiah, the Branch, the living Christ and a former carpenter skilled in crafting wood who will build the true future Messianic temple which has been so clearly prophesied in Scripture.

From all around the world, people will come to help our Lord in this divinely ordained construction project, and it is from this Millennial temple that Jesus will rule and reign from His throne.

In the following section of this book, we will explore what that throne may be. Yes, I believe the throne where Christ will sit and rule may actually exist today. And if it truly does, as I suspect, then it is hidden away in the most unsuspecting place on the planet.

If what you have read so far hasn't given a paradigm jolt to your mind, then what you are about to discover will give you acute intellectual whiplash!

Part III

The Ark of the Covenant and the Millennial Temple

CHAPTER 15

SEARCHING FOR THE ARK

I realize that the temple re-location has already strayed far afield from the limits of most traditional comfort zones. So it is with utmost caution that I take one more step into the dark corridors of history and again lift a candle into the past—that we may possibly better understand our way into the future.

It seems to me that the elusive Ark of the Covenant holds many secrets involving the temple being in the City of David as well as how it involves Christ's millennial reign in that temple.

What I am about to share is a synopsis of my many years of research in Ethiopia searching for the ark. If it has somehow survived to this day, I feel the Ark of the Covenant is of incalculable importance for what lies ahead. I believe that beyond all counterintuitive reasoning that the ark/mercy seat may be intact, and that it could be a cornerstone of prophetic relevancy including how it fits into the new temple location.

The research on the theory presented here is that the Ark of the Covenant has possibly survived and is in Ethiopia, but also that Jesus Christ will rule and reign from the golden mercy seat in the millennial reign.

PERSONAL JOURNEYS

The theory of the throne started for me on a beautiful spring morning several years ago in the foothills of Colorado Springs, Colorado. The columbines strained up through the newly thawed ground. The smell of pine sap filled the air and mixed with the scent of the loamy forest outside my open office window. I heard a car door slam and saw Ken Durham coming up the walk to my office. A lone deer grazing in a nearby patch of old scrub-oak took notice of him as well, and scampered off. The bespectacled instructor with salt-and-pepper hair entered my office and sat down. Ken was assistant professor of biblical studies at a Christian college in Colorado. For several months prior, Ken had heard about my many trips to Ethiopia on the theory that the Ark of the Covenant was legend to be in a small chapel known as the Saint Mary of Zion Church in the northern city of Axum.

With that information, Ken said that he had a theory of his own and that if the ark was still in Ethiopia then it had to have a prophetic obligation. He believed there was more than a coincidence that so many biblical verses come to light when he put a lens of possibility on Ethiopia as the place God chose to keep the ark. His theory blew me away, but to have it make any sense, let me share my personal journeys to this distant land. Perhaps we will be able to see how the ark in Ethiopia and the temple being moved to the city of David harmonizes with each other in a stunning way.

GONE WITHOUT A TRACE?

After all these centuries, there is a deep reverence toward the Ark of the Covenant in the Judeo-Christian world. The Bible refers to the ark more than two hundred times. From the days of Moses to the reign of Solomon, it played a prominent, even profound role in the history of early Israel. But then, for reasons that still baffle scholars and theologians alike, its story simply ends. To most, the ark is gone without a trace and without even a verifiable suggestion as to where it may be. But there are some with a different opinion.

In Ethiopia today, you can hardly find a single individual out of a population of ninety million who harbors the slightest doubt that the ark lies quietly in state in a chapel at Axum. From the lowliest peasant to the highest public official, all insist that, secured within the shadows of Saint Mary of Zion's fortified inner sanctum, separated from the outside world only by a high iron fence and a lonely guardian, sits a wooden chest of superb biblical significance. It is interesting to pause here and note that Ethiopia is the only country in the world making the claim that they truly have the actual Ark of the Covenant from Old Testament days.

I have personally traveled to Ethiopia twenty times and have written two books on the theory of the ark surviving in the small town of Axum—if it can even be called a town. It lies in the rugged, dust-dry highlands of north-central Ethiopia. Once the center of a powerful kingdom rivaling the mightiest nations of the ancient past, Axum today is little more than a dusty village decaying into obscurity. Lying some 200 miles inland from the Red Sea coast, it looks little different from dozens of other mud-hut villages strewn across Ethiopia's rugged Abyssinian Highlands.

Yet Axum is different.

At the center of town sits the famed Chapel of Saint Mary of Zion, the most venerated of the country's more than twenty thousand churches and monasteries. Strange as it may seem, this humble structure lays claim to housing the original ark as described in the Bible.

Words on a page can't begin to convey the ark's incalculable value to the Judeo-Christian world. This plum of archaeology —crafted at Mount Sinai of acacia wood, overlaid with gold, sent wandering in the wilderness, and eventually placed in Solomon's temple—not only provided a sacred repository of the Ten Commandments (the moral code of law and justice governing every civilized society since), but it also reportedly channeled the power to stop mighty rivers, lay waste to walled cities, wipe out armies, and certify kingdoms.

The heavenly instructions on how to build the ark were placed in the hands of master craftsmen at Mount Sinai with skills worthy of the Divine. The base material of the box and poles were wood, commonly called acacia wood. These areas were laminated with a veneer of gold. The ark was two and a half cubits in length and one and a half in width [loosely 52 inches by 31 inches]. There were four rings of gold at the base that held the wooden carrying poles which were laminated in gold as well. The ark was capped with a hammered gold lid called the mercy seat. Some say that the mercy seat was a throne of pure gold with two hammered (low-profiled) cherubim with outstretched wings, which were positioned on the top of the mercy seat.

The ark possessed unimaginable powers. And more profound, God spoke to Moses above the mercy seat, between the cherubim. People shuddered in its presence. It was feared, worshiped, and sought after. Precise instructions as to its use were given to Moses and severe catastrophe would ensue if strict protocol was violated in the least.

After the Ark of the Covenant was created at Mount Sinai, it was then housed in an elaborate portable residence called the tabernacle, or tent. On leaving Sinai, the ark wandered in the wilderness for forty years and eventually came to Jerusalem where it was placed in a tabernacle by David. The ark was eventually housed in the magnificent temple of Solomon, but it subsequently disappeared in history after 701 BC.

PICKS, SHOVELS, AND RIOTS

It was not untill 1867 that the ark was pursued once more when a young lieutenant assigned to Britain's Royal Engineers cut a tunnel under the exterior walls of the Temple Mount thinking the ark was hidden somewhere beneath. In a clandestine maneuver to secure the ark, the clamor of sledgehammers and pickaxes below the Al-Aqsa Mosque disturbed the prayers of the Muslim faithful who gathered top-side. The event triggered a hail of stones ending in a bloody riot.

Many years later, in 1910, another Englishman, Montague Brownslow Parker, paid hefty bribes to gain secret access to the southern part of the Temple Mount (where the ark was legend to still exist). An excavation ensued, in which Parker and his team used ropes lashed to the *Shetiyyah*, or foundation stone, to lower themselves into the Well of Souls. Yet once again, the racket alerted a mosque attendant, who, inspecting the ruckus, recoiled to see foreigners hacking at holy ground with picks and shovels. He sounded the alarm, bringing enraged Muslim vigilantes racing to the scene. The explorers fled Jerusalem with an angry mob at their heels.[1]

For religious Jews—who look to the discovery of the Ark of the Covenant under the Temple Mount as a prophetic signpost of Israel's return to splendor—it seems tragic (and a bit ironic) that, in an era of technology that might lend itself to successful exploration of the Temple Mount, opportunities to explore do not exist for very obvious reasons. Muslims, who control the Temple Mount, as stated earlier, would make any such search untenable.

Nonetheless, modern interest in the ark received a sharp spike some years ago with the popularity of the movie, *Raiders of the Lost Ark,* which—while offering little in the way of biblical accuracy—served to refocus attention on this unique item of Old Testament significance. One result of this upsurge seems to have been the re-emergence of theories and guesses concerning the whereabouts of the Ark of the Covenant—if indeed it exists at all today.

Other popular theories suggesting the hiding place for the ark are found in 2 Maccabees 2:5, which proposes that it was hidden by Jeremiah in a cave on Mount Nebo (in modern day Jordan).

Jewish archaeologists have done their best to follow this as a valid lead, but to date no evidence has emerged that would indicate it is any more than a legend.

Another source suggested that King Shishak of Egypt had looted the temple and stolen treasures of gold and silver. This theory was the basis for the movie *Raiders of the Lost Ark.* Another further speculation is that King Nebuchadnezzar of Babylonia destroyed the ark when he invaded Israel in 598 BC.

FOLLOWING THE TRAIL

Today, in Ethiopia, the monks claim they have the ark under their protection and warn that no one but the Guardian of the Ark is allowed to lay eyes upon it. The guardian is a spiritual man selected from the priests and assigned to spend his entire life in worshipful solitude, guarding the ark. He will never leave the small fenced chapel of Saint Mary of Zion Church until he is carried away for his funeral.

The route of the ark to Ethiopia, however, can be easily traced like a trail of historical bread crumbs. The last known reference to the ark's presence in the temple was during Hezekiah's reign. Hezekiah went up to the temple (701 BC) and prayed, *"O Lord God of Israel, the One who dwells between the cherubim, You are God, You alone, of all the kingdoms of the earth. You have made heaven and earth"* (2 Kings 19:15).

Because the Bible declares that the Lord dwells between the cherubim, and Hezekiah was praying to the Lord, whose manifested presence appeared above the ark, it can be deduced that the ark was in residence in the temple. However, it was missing from the temple prior to Josiah's reign (three kings after Hezekiah). We know this because Josiah spoke to his priests, saying, *"Put the holy Ark in the Temple that was built by Solomon son of David, the king of Israel. You no longer need to carry it back and forth on your shoulders, Now spend your time serving the Lord your God and his people Israel.* (2 Chronicles 35:3 NLT).

The verb "put" in this verse may be a clue that the ark was not in the temple at that time. If the ark was already resting in the temple, why would Josiah ask the priests to *put* it there? When he says, *"It shall no longer be a burden on your shoulders,"* this may indicate that the ark was being carried from place to place, far from Jerusalem.

Only two kings reigned between Hezekiah and Josiah: Manasseh (687-642 BC) and Amon (642-640 BC). Amon was assassinated after only two years as king, and he was replaced by his son, who had a long and wicked reign. Manasseh will always be remembered as a king who did evil in the sight of the Lord. He is the person most likely responsible for allowing the Ark of the Covenant to slip away from Solomon's temple. He is the perfect villain in this ancient mystery and it was on Manasseh that I would zero in.

Here is what Scripture tells us:

> *"He rebuilt the pagan shrines his father, Hezekiah, had destroyed. He constructed altars for Baal and set up an*

> *Asherah pole, just as King Ahab of Israel had done. He also bowed before all the powers of the heavens and worshiped them. He built pagan altars in the Temple of the Lord, the place where the Lord had said, 'My name will remain in Jerusalem forever.' He built these altars for all the powers of the heavens in both courtyards of the Lord's Temple.*
>
> *Manasseh also sacrificed his own son in the fire. He practiced sorcery and divination, and he consulted with mediums and psychics. He did much that was evil in the Lord's sight, arousing his anger. Manasseh even made a carved image of Asherah and set it up in the Temple, the very place where the Lord had told David and his son Solomon: 'My name will be honored forever in this Temple and in Jerusalem—the city I have chosen from among all the tribes of Israel....'*
>
> *Manasseh also murdered many innocent people until Jerusalem was filled from one end to the other with innocent blood. This was in addition to the sin that he caused the people of Judah to commit, leading them to do evil in the Lord's sight"* (2 Kings 21:3-7,16, NLT).

There is no doubt that old Manasseh was the scum of the earth. As a result of his loathsome actions, God pronounced a grave sentence on Israel. He removed His hand from the nation —and very likely, the ark was removed as well, because it was during his time that the ark is said to have arrived on Elephantine Island in Egypt. The priests would have been repulsed by all that Manasseh did and perhaps hid or removed the ark to avoid any further defilement.

DID GOD USE PHARAOH?

The Bible gives subtle clues that the ark may have been taken to Egypt. In 2 Chronicles 35, we are told that Josiah prepared the temple (even though the ark was gone). *"Prepare"* (verse 6) here is the same as preparing your home for visitors, and awkwardly in the same passage, Josiah goes out to battle Neco, the Pharaoh of

Egypt. This makes no sense at all. Josiah had no clear reason to do so; in fact it is puzzling why he would pick such a fight. Neco, confused by Josiah's weird behavior, had sent messengers warning him to stay away and leave him alone.

Neco's ambassadors asked, *"What do you want with me, king of Judah? I have no quarrel with you today! I am on my way to fight another nation, and God has told me to hurry! Do not interfere with God, who is with me, or He will destroy you"* (2 Chronicles 35:21, NLT).

A close look reveals some amazing insights as to what was really going on behind the scenes. This verse actually is saying that Pharaoh was taking orders directly from the God of Israel.

Pharaoh Neco is clearly warning Josiah as well as scolding him. The New King James Version reads, *"Refrain from meddling with God, who is with me, lest He destroy you"* (2 Chronicles 35:21).

In Hebrew, the statement doesn't just mean, "God is on my side." Rather, the preposition indicates that the Almighty was literally with Neco—physically, in his company, and in his very presence. It is a dramatic statement that goes almost unnoticed in the Bible, but Neco informs Josiah that the God of the Hebrews is with him, personally on-site! This remarkable nugget of dialogue reveals two crucial points: Neco had received his orders directly from God, and the Lord was somehow actually present with Neco. The larger question is, *was the ark with him as well?*

It seems that the ark had to be with Neco for Josiah to do such strange things. The young king would have been under incredible political pressure from his priests to retrieve the ark at all costs. It seems a fair bet that Josiah did risk his life to get the ark back from Pharaoh. In 2 Chronicles 35:22, we read that Josiah *"refused to listen to Neco, to whom God had indeed spoken."*

This is not a quote from Neco, but from the scribe who wrote 2 Chronicles, stating that Neco was receiving his instructions directly from the mouth of God (or the Lord's manifest presence). God spoke to Moses from above the mercy seat, and He may have spoken to Neco in the very same way.

Josiah decided to disguise himself so the enemy would not recognize him. He died by an arrow's impact and the ark went on its prophetic journey.

There are three important points to be learned from all this:

First: The ark remained in the temple during the reign of Hezekiah, who prayed to God "who dwells between the cherubim."

Second: The ark was absent from the temple during the reign of Josiah (the Levites carried it on their shoulders to an unknown location).

Third: Therefore, the ark most likely disappeared during the reign of Manasseh (or possibly during the rule of Amon, Manasseh's son, who ruled for two years before being assassinated) and was transported to Egypt by loyal Levites.

"A STRONG CONVICTION"

In the earlier years of my ark search, I flew to Israel to interview the black Ethiopian Jews now living there as well as expert Shalva Weil. I really didn't know how I would find the Ethiopian Jews that were scattered in Israel, but I simply took a cab and went to the Western Wailing Wall and there I found several Jewish men from the Gondor region on Lake T'ana. In 1984 the Israeli government airlifted them to Jerusalem along with 10,000 other Falashas during a mission called "Operation Moses."

After asking point blank about the ark, they all told me with toothy wide grins that, for sure, the Ark of the Covenant was in a church in Axum. The Falasha religious leaders there also confirmed that for 200 years the ark was in Egypt before continuing south to T'ana Kirkos Island. After another 800 years, the ark was moved from T'ana Kirkos to Axum by the Ethiopian King Ezana, and I was emphatically informed that it remains there to this day.

I then visited the Jerusalem Hebrew Institute, where I interviewed social anthropologist Dr. Weil to see if a historical record exists of Ethiopian Jews possessing the ark. She was a no-nonsense scholar who spoke in measured words as if she were delivering one of her thousands of lectures. She described the Ethiopian Falasha Jews as modern descendants of Old Testament Hebrews who traveled to Egypt centuries ago. After settling in Egypt for a time, she said, they made their way south through Nubia (southern Egypt and northern Sudan), and eventually occupied northern Ethiopia.

When I asked about the possibility that the Ark of the Covenant was taken by these Jews and was now resting in the chapel at Axum, she smiled, drew a deep breath, and replied, "There is a very strong conviction that the Ethiopian Christians possess the ark."

Chapter 16

The Secrets of Egypt and Ethiopia

From Israel, I flew to Egypt to visit Elephantine Island, where archaeologists had unearthed evidence of an ancient Hebrew temple from the time of King Manasseh.

The only way to reach the island however was by a sail boat called a *felluca*. I hired a young Egyptian to take me across the Nile and, after pushing off from the dock, the shifting wind bloated the sails and the sleek craft glided its way through the green lethargic current with ease. I enjoyed the gurgling sound as the Nile gently massaged the wooden hull, and within a few minutes, the squeaky wooden tiller in the lad's skilled hand guided us perfectly to the island's rocky edge.

I stepped from the boat and followed a walking path to an austere grey-concrete museum. It was filled with shelves of pottery and ancient musty-smelling stuff that did not interest me. The only thing I wanted to know about was an old wooden box with gold overlay that may have been at this exact spot more than 2,000 years ago.

A Muslim woman with a black silk scarf tied around her face sat behind a leaning wooden desk. She smiled warmly and I asked, "Can anyone tell me about the Ark of the Covenant ever being on this island?"

She tilted her head, perhaps surprised by the unusual question. After a short moment she said softy, "I will get for you Dr. Hanna."

She walked to the door of an office and spoke to whoever was inside, then pointed at me. A small Egyptian man in his forties emerged fom the office.

"Yes, what is your question, please?" His tone was formal but hurried.

"I was wondering if you could tell me if the Ark of the Covenant had ever been on this island."

He held out his hand and said, "Let me introduce myself. I am Dr. Atif Hanna with the Institute of Cairo Coptic Studies." He had a thin face and nose that donned a pronounced bushy moustache.

I introduced myself, and with my forearm I wiped off beads of sweat encouraged by a high arching noonday sun. I explained that I was researching the history of the Ark of the Covenant. "Do you know anything about the ark? Was it ever on this island?"

Dr. Hanna said nothing, but waved for me to follow him. We left the museum and strolled up a dirt path to a rounded hilltop. Tunnels honeycombed the area and toppled statues and columns littered the ground. It looked like a graveyard of broken stones that were once magnificent edifices.

Dr. Hanna sat down on a carved rock. He looked skyward; apparently netting his thoughts, then gave a short dissertation in an Egyptian accent as thick as tar.

He began, "The Ark of the Covenant moved from Jerusalem at the time of King Manasseh and came to Elephantine Island. Yes, the Ark of the Covenant remained here for some time at the Jewish temple. At the third century before Christ, some of the Jewish community moved south to keep it...to Abyssinia or Ethiopia...and the Ark of the Covenant is still until now in that area."

He then told me about papyrus scrolls and potsherds that were dug from the sand at Elephantine that were written by Hebrews in Aswan to those in Jerusalem in the mid-seventh century. The writings referred to the "temple of Yahweh" used to shelter the "Person of God."

Dr. Hanna looked across the sluggish green Nile and said the Hebrews built a replica temple on the island about 650 BC, during the reign of Judah's King Manasseh and hostile Egyptians destroyed it. He returned his gaze, "Perhaps the Jews' sacrifice of rams was one reason for this, because it was the image of an Egyptian god. After 200 years, in approximately 410 BC, the whole Hebrew community mysteriously vanished."

A JEWISH TEMPLE IN EGYPT

I already knew that some scholars believed that the community on Elephantine consisted of Hebrew mercenaries; others thought it was a mix of refugees, including Levitical priests seeking sanctuary from the wicked King Manasseh's persecution.

Could this Elephantine temple have been modeled after the first temple in Jerusalem? Was it a temporary resting place for the ark? Though building such a temple on Egyptian soil would have been a serious violation of Israelite law, which forbade constructing a temple or offering sacrifices outside of Jerusalem, it may have been rationalized because of Manasseh's evil excesses. In any event, the Elephantine Hebrews clearly thought that Yahweh had resided physically in their temple. A number of papyri speak of Yahweh as "dwelling" there.[1]

If such a temple were built to house the ark, it helps explain the ark's disappearance from Jerusalem in the early-to-mid-600s BC, and why it didn't arrive in Ethiopia until approximately 800 years later.

Dr. Hanna continued, "In 525 BC, a Persian king invaded Egypt and proceeded to torch many Egyptian temples, but, interestingly, he did not touch a single stone on the Jewish temple at Elephantine. The invader's name was Cambyses, the son of Cyrus the Great, who ordered that the building should begin on Zerubbabel's temple at Jerusalem."

The huge question is: *why was Elephantine spared his wrath?* Could it be that the same Persian King Cyrus who ordered the temple rebuilt in Jerusalem, knew that the ark was in another Jewish temple on a small island in Egypt where I was now standing?

"The ark was never mentioned in the Bible again," Dr. Hanna told me with a halting manner, "because it came here to the Jewish temple at Elephantine."

The Jewish refugees constructed a temple whose dimensions and appearance—exterior pillars, gateways of stone, roof of cedar wood—were modeled precisely on Solomon's temple. Papyrus records indicate that the Hebrews performed ritual animal sacrifices at the Elephantine temple just as in Jerusalem, including the all-important sacrifice of a lamb during Passover. It seems that the Elephantine temple of Yahweh was destroyed in 410 BC, within sixty years of the date that legend says the ark arrived in Ethiopia (around 470 BC).

THE "HOLY ISLAND"

If the Ark of the Covenant was moved from Egypt to Ethiopia, I wanted to learn all I could about one of its possible resting places. A destination called Lake T'ana, in Ethiopia, held many secrets, and I wanted to discover more. It is the largest lake in the nation—about 50 miles across—located in the northwest Ethiopian highlands. The lake has several islands, many home to monasteries and churches.

After a slow boat trip of over three hours, we reached T'ana Kirkos, called a "holy island," inhabited only by monks. It is believed by many Ethiopians that the Ark of the Covenant resided here after being moved from Egypt.

The island had tall cliffs, crowned with primeval trees and towering cactus. The captain then slowly steered the boat into a shady, placid lagoon. As he pulled close to the orange-colored rocks, I saw a narrow flight of granite steps chiseled into the cliff. A six-foot long lizard didn't like us being there and dove from the steps and into a patch of lily pads leaving a trailing line of disappearing bubbles.

Some old monks of the Ethiopian Church met us as we tied-off and I was soon hiking along a narrow trail to meet the chief priest, Abba (meaning *father*). He was wearing a flowing white robe and jungle-stained turban. He stooped in the narrow, vegetation-canopied path as we approached, and looked as if he were an immovable root from an ancient tree.

But after some conversational exchanges, courtesy of my guide, Misgana, the Abba bowed slightly. His outstretched right hand then shook mine, while holding my wrist with his left—a gesture of honor. The priest led us up the overgrown path through an ancient stone archway and into a mosquito-infested grassy clearing. There we saw a couple of dilapidated shacks and a few raggedly dressed monks. The holy men who walked nearby seemed oblivious to our presence.

We would eventually be taken to the cliff area to set up camp. The mosquitos were just too pesky anywhere else. Our lashed-down tent was precariously balanced on the spine of a high ridge. Other than the feeling we might roll off the sheer cliffs, we were thankful for a fresh breeze that blew in off the lake, bringing a blue wisp of clouds across a misty full moon. Surrounded by palm fronds, enveloped in soft trickles of cook smoke from the monks below, it seemed as if I'd been edited into an African Safari movie.

UNDER THE ENCRUSTED MOSS

Sleep came quick and in the thick hazy morning air, Abba awakened us, and we were led to a narrow path bordered by prickly, overgrown bushes. A series of rough stone steps emptied out onto a narrow plateau at the island's summit. The view of the glistening jade lake and surrounding verdant jungle was magnificent.

With Misgana interpreting, the Abba told us, "This is where the ritual blood sacrifices took place centuries ago by the Jewish caretakers of the ark."

Near the ledge stood a lichen-covered block of granite with a six-inch squared hole carved in its top. From the thick layer of encrusted moss on it, the stone was hundreds, possibly thousands of years old.

Abba walked over and demonstrated how the holes in the columns had been used to collect blood during the ritual sacrifice of the lamb. Holding up an imaginary basin to illustrate how the ancient priests scattered blood over the stones, Abba pretended to pour the remaining blood into the hollows in the pillars.

In both size and shape, the columns resembled the stone *masseboth* set up on high places in the earliest phases of the

Hebrew religion. These ritual altars had served for sacrificial offering ceremonies much as Abba described.[2]

Abba showed us how the high priest dipped his right forefinger into a basin containing the blood, then scattered it over the stones and tent in an up-and-down, whip-like motion. He made a tipping movement, as if pouring blood from the imaginary basin into the cup-shaped hollows of the pillars.

The manner in which he reenacted the sacrament seemed to mimic purification rites prescribed in the Old Testament book of Leviticus: 4 and 5.

The granite altar did indeed seem appropriate to the ancient Hebrew ritual. But where did the ark fit in? Where did it sit beneath the tabernacle? I knew the monks had never revealed to any outsider precisely where the ark had sat on the island. The best they could offer renowned British author and explorer, Graham Hancock, was that it lay "somewhere near" the cliffs where we now stood.[3]

With nothing to lose, I decided to ask: "Abba, where did the ark sit?"

My heart skipped a beat when he casually lifted his calloused ebony finger and pointed to the smooth granite beneath my feet.

"The ark sat right here?" I asked, looking down.

"Yes," he nodded slowly with the slight trace of a smile.

He explained, and Misgana relayed the words in English. "He says the ark sat here, on this ledge, so that the blood could also be sprinkled on the tabernacle at the time of the sacrifice. This tradition has been passed down through the centuries."

THE SOCKET HOLES

This confused me since the Bible makes no mention of sprinkling blood on the tabernacle.

I stared at the smooth surface of rock, perched high above the lagoon and surrounded on all sides by sheer cliffs. As a formidable watchtower from which to repel invaders, the ledge made perfect sense. I bent down to inspect the granite surface, an unremarkable table of stone covered in decaying leaves and layers of thatch.

I then got down on my knees and began poking around, pushing leaves and thatch aside and feeling for something—I wasn't sure what. I took out my knife and slid it down through the thick thatch, poking and prodding, sticking it into rocks and cracks, searching for a spot where the granite might yield to emptiness.

After some digging there was a socket hole, hidden beneath centuries of decayed organic matter, where workers could anchor a tent pole securing the tabernacle that held the ark. I began clearing the rest of the ledge, probing the leaves and debris with my knife. After some minor excavation, I found a second hole, roughly the same circumference as the first. Six inches of rotting palm fronds had been covering it. While not quite as pronounced as the first, this one sat closer to the ledge and appeared to have been eroded by wind, rain, and time.

I scoured the rest of the slab but never found the other two tent holes. By the look of the ledge, the rock where the other holes would have been carved had fallen off or worn away by the jungle's harsh hand of erosion.

I noticed a small pile of rocks stacked next to the altar—a makeshift shrine? Among the chunks sat a sizeable piece of granite with a tent pole-sized hole carved in the top. By appearances, it might have been a third socket hole, long since broken away from the ledge.

After our time exploring, we walked back down the trail as my mind swirled with provocative scenarios. Had we just stood on the *Shetiyyah* of T'ana Kirkos, the foundation stone of an ancient Ethiopian Holy of Holies?

Had I hollowed out the contours of the tent holes that had once supported the tabernacle of the ark? I noticed Abba eying me with some interest, his expression registering an uneasy tension at the discovery of the possible tent-peg holes locations, as if he had never seen them.

"I don't really think they knew the holes were there," Misgana whispered.

Back at the village, Abba led us to a thick-walled mud hut and unlocked heavy wooden doors. He disappeared inside the darkened room for a moment.

"I believe the elder has something else to show you," Misgana said.

Emerging a few minutes later, Abba placed a small grass mat on the ground for us to sit on. He laid another mat a few feet in front of us. Then he instructed someone to help him carry over a large basin. It was broad and shallow, approximately two feet wide, and no more than a couple of inches deep. A green patina from many years of oxidation made it difficult for me to identify the metal. I guessed that it was bronze and it looked as if it had been in existence for several millennia.

Abba explained, "The ancient Hebrews who brought the ark to Lake T'ana called it a *gomer*. They used it up on the cliffs to collect the blood used in the ritual sacrifices. The priest would stir the blood in the basin to keep it from getting thick."

THE METAL STAND

Abba reentered the storage hut and returned, balancing a heavy, bulky tangle of metal in his hands. It was a single stand of what appeared to be rusted-through iron rods fused to a ring at the top and bottom. Abba told us that it had once been a sturdy stand to hold the bronze bowl. It looked to me as if it had long since collapsed from metal fatigue and extreme age. Its edges were mottled and encrusted with the same aged pits and corrosion as the bowl, but it had a deep, red-brown oxidation.

The opening at the top of the stand seemed to be about the same dimensions as the bronze basin, so it made sense that this was the stand for the bronze bowl.

Cradling the basin like a newborn baby, Abba again described how his predecessors had used it to scatter blood in the ancient Hebrew fashion. Yet the more I looked, the more the basin and stand seemed to reflect passages in Exodus and Leviticus describing "basin and stand" as an integrated unit for ritual cleansing (Exodus 30:17-19). Or it could have held the sacred anointing oil used to consecrate "the Tent of Meeting" (Exodus

30:28-29). Both basin and stand also appear in Leviticus, when Moses ordained Aaron and his sons for the priesthood (Leviticus 8:10-11). But Abba and his predecessors interpreted the basin as an instrument for blood sacrifice. It didn't really matter. These implements possibly shared a Hebrew origin, and the monks on T'ana Kirkos had neither the resources nor the technology to forge metal. Someone had obviously brought them here.

I thought of the silver trumpets at the Axum chapel and wondered if this basin and stand had been among the original temple vessels, forged in Moses' time and placed in Solomon's temple for service before the ark. Had these instruments actually come to T'ana Kirkos with the ark?

The Monks insisted that they had, but I assumed they might have been replicas made long ago. If they are forged in the image of the temple implements, they may offer a rare picture of the temple's distant past.

MEAT FORKS AND ALMOND BUDS

Abba reemerged from the hut holding a long, two-pronged instrument that looked like two long thin spears fastened together. I quickly identified it as consistent with yet another Hebrew sacrificial implement, a meat fork used to burn sacrifices over ritual fires.

"Abba says it is a meat fork," Misgana said, "left on the island by those who brought the ark."

The top, I was soon told, was shaped as a budding almond flower. My mind drifted back to Saudi Arabia and the mountain called Jabal al-Lawz, which in English means "mountain of the almond flower."

Throughout the Old Testament, the budding almond ranked high in Israel's sacred iconography, adorning many vessels used in the Tent of Meeting and in the first temple (Exodus 25:33-34; 37:19-20).

One of the noted Bible stories is of Aaron's almond wood staff miraculously budding overnight (Numbers 17:8). That same staff, regarded as the sign of one of Yahweh's great Old Testament miracles, came to lie alongside the holy manna and the Ten Commandments within the Ark of the Covenant (Hebrews 9:4).

If I had only seen one or two of these artifacts, I might have written it off as coincidence. Yet taken together—the cliff shrine, the pillars for blood sacrifice, the hidden tent holes, and now the basin, stand, and meat fork—we seemed to have uncovered interlocking pieces of a fantastic puzzle. Each of these vessels and components appeared much like those described in Scripture; each made an arguable case for T'ana Kirkos as an ancient Hebrew haven; and each suggested at least the possibility that this might have been a resting place for the Ark of the Covenant.

A 1,700-year-old parchment book was brought out and opened. The pages were cracked, weathered and discolored by being bathed for a millennium and three quarters in candle smoke. The Abba handled the book with careful slow movements as if he were holding a dry butterfly wing. He almost whispered, "This is a painting of the tabernacle tent that held the ark on our island."

The final page was slowly turned and the still dried animal skin page crinkled. Then, there it was! An ancient faded and bug-eaten page that showed the tabernacle tent that the monks said with holy reverence once held the ark on the rock ledge I had stood upon.

The monks on the island told me that in 338 AD, the ark was taken from T'ana Kirkos island by Christian convert King Ezana to Axum, Ethiopia. The ark allegedly rests in total dark isolation today in Saint Mary of Zion Church, under the protection of a lone "Guardian of the Ark." Absolutely no one is allowed to see the ark except for the Guardian.

THE RESTING PLACE?

I had been to Axum earlier in that week and found the place just as funky as being on this mysterious island. At the center of this town sits a simple thick-walled chapel that Ethiopians claim holds perhaps the greatest secret in history, the resting place of the Ark of the Covenant.

It may be hard for many to ever believe that this dusty patch of dirt holds a holy artifact of immense proportions. Why would God ever choose this struggling population of hard-pressed humanity as custodial keepers of the ark? But this poor city was once the center of a lavish, powerful kingdom. Axum is said to have rivaled the mightiest nations of the ancient past. The city was once the capital of a powerful kingdom that dominated the crossroads of Africa and Asia for a thousand years. The first reports of this highly developed civilization are from 64 AD, when the Greek author Periplus described Axum's ruler as "a prince superior to most and educated with knowledge of Greek." Centuries later, a Roman ambassador named Julian glowingly described Axum as "the greatest city of all of Ethiopia."

Axum's king wore the finest of linen garments embroidered with strands of gold from his waist to his loins, and he rode a four-wheeled, elephant-drawn chariot shingled with solid gold plates. They minted their own coins in Axum, and merchants traveled to India, Ceylon, and as far away as China. This culture adopted Christianity during the fourth century and now lays claim to possess a great archaeological prize.

Ethiopians maintain that no one will ever see what they insist is the Ark of the Covenant. They say that what is in their care is so holy that only one man—the Guardian of the Ark—is worthy of even seeing it. The guardian is a spiritual man selected from the priests and assigned to spend his entire life in worshipful solitude, worshiping and protecting the ark.

QUESTIONS FOR THE KEEPER

When I was finally allowed to meet the guardian at Saint Mary of Zion Church on a subsequent trip, he struck me as a typically bone-thin Ethiopian, wearing only slightly more elaborate robes than the other monks. His wordly name was Abba Mekonen, and was known as Atang, or the "Keeper of the Ark." He had a full beard, soft eyes, and a warm, if melancholy, smile. I knew I had been afforded a rare honor.

The Atang seldom appears in public, and as the most revered priest of the Ethiopian Orthodox Church, he *never* leaves the small chapel compound. He is a self-imposed prisoner of his own spiritual virtues, willing to serve the remainder of his life here in pious worship of what he believes is the actual Ark of the Covenant.

Before being allowed to ask questions, the Atang prayed a blessing over me, and sprinkled my head with holy water from a tarnished pewter chalice. He then gently placed his silver cross on my forehead, cheeks, and lips. Startled villagers pressed in around, seeming agitated, even angered, to see their holy man lavishing blessings on a white foreigner.

I eased into the conversation by introducing myself and explaining why I had come to Axum. As I spoke I recall looking into the Atang's eyes and thought to myself that there was almost a sadness reflecting from his stare. What a sacrifice he has made by becoming the guardian. He will never again be able to walk the hills of his youth, or be able to linger on long summer afternoons with friends and family! The Atang had lived a virtuous life, and for that he now ministered before an object that he—and others—believed to be an instrument of God's ineffable will.

With a gentleness I found remarkable, even for a man of the Atang's spiritual capacities, he said he had long ago made peace with his fate. "It is not for my own happiness," he said, "but for God's pleasure that I occupy this position."

At last I posed the question I'd been longing to ask: "Honored guardian, I have come to ask you in person: Do you truly guard the original Ark of the Covenant?"

"Yes," he said, "we have the ark."

"May I ask what it *looks* like?" His well-rehearsed answer echoed similar accounts I'd read.

"As it is described in the Bible, so it is," he said mechanically. "King Solomon placed the ark in the Holy of Holies of the temple that he had built in Jerusalem. From there it was removed and brought to Ethiopia."

As I prepared to ask him specifically about its features—the configuration of the cherubim, its exact dimensions—the Atang raised a hand, halting all questions. With a small trace of a smile he politely excused himself, bowed lightly, then turned to walk back up the steps into the chapel.

My session with the guardian had ended as suddenly as it had begun, but there would be many more times I would come to see him over the years and each time I greet the Guardian, he now calls me *son*. He also always gives me the same answers when asking about the ark, so any such questions have been halted. But I enjoy seeing him very much and I always look deep into his eyes that are tarnished a yellowish-brown from years of exposure to wafting incense smoke. I think to myself, *these tired eyes may have actually gazed upon the real Ark of the Covenant.*

So, is the ark in Ethiopia, do we have the real proof? The end of the matter is simply this: if what lies in Axum is the true ark, then God's protective hand is upon it. It will not be moved, seen, or touched before its time. God will do what God will do, directing events for His own pleasure, at His own discretion, to His own ends—sometimes in cooperation with, but usually in spite of, what humans think or do.

CHAPTER 17

THE GLORIOUS RETURN TO THE TEMPLE

In chapter 15, I mentioned my discussions with professor Ken Durham regarding the Ark of the Covenant possibly being in Ethiopia. This was long before I ever considered an alternative site of the temples. Back then I brought Ken a passage of Scripture that I had been brooding over. I didn't know it at the time, but the verses would lead to a surprising theory in biblical prophecy.

Isaiah 18 sounds like a travelogue of northern Ethiopia. The passage reads:

> *"Woe to the land of whirring wings along the rivers of Cush, which sends envoys by sea in papyrus boats over the water. Go, swift messengers, to a people tall and smooth-skinned, to a people feared far and wide, an aggressive nation of strange speech, whose land is divided by rivers...At that time gifts will be brought to the Lord Almighty from a people tall and smooth-skinned, from a people feared far and wide, an aggressive nation of strange speech, whose land is divided by rivers—the gifts will be brought to Mount Zion, the place of the Name of the Lord Almighty"* (Isaiah 18:1-2,7 NIV).

I recognized these verses as a prophecy to the ancient land of

Ethiopia, although prophetic to *what,* I couldn't say. *Cush* is a Hebrew term referring to a nebulous territory that had, in the earliest Greek editions of the Bible, been translated as *Ethiopia.* In fact, many new translations use *Ethiopia* instead of *Cush.*

The Greek word *Ethiopia* means "burnt faces," while the Hebrew term *Cush* referred to the entire Nile Valley south of Egypt, including Nubia and Abyssinia.[1]

Today, most scholars agree that Cush applies only to the northern half of modern Ethiopia. It is from this land that Moses took a wife (Numbers 21:1).

I held these Isaiah 18 verses with particular interest. With its rich imagery of papyrus boats and smooth-skinned natives, it seemed an accurate picture of the land I would come to love. I knew Ethiopia could easily qualify as a place of "whirring wings." Swarms of ever-present flies and mosquitoes molest everyone in northern Ethiopia. Likewise, Cush's "papyrus boats" conjured up images of the Ethiopian *tankwas,* or papyrus canoes, made by the shoreline natives of Lake T'ana even to this day.

The Ethiopians I had observed were indeed tall and smooth-skinned, with glowing, chestnut-brown complexions. No one could dispute that it is a country "divided by rivers," crisscrossing the mountainous land in the Horn of Africa. I had seen both the roaring Atbara and Tekezé rivers cutting a glistening swath through hot, rocky highlands.

What, exactly, did Isaiah mean when he predicted, "At that time *gifts* will be brought to the Lord Almighty from a people tall and smooth-skinned...the *gifts* will be brought to Mount Zion, the place of the Name of the Lord Almighty" (Isaiah 18:7)? It appeared from this verse that *something* prophetic would happen in Ethiopia that would directly impact Jerusalem, and more specifically Mount Zion (temple location).

I asked Ken again, "What gifts will the Ethiopians bring to the Lord?"

"First," the professor began, "like so many sections of Isaiah, this is God's message to a specific region and its people. Messages like this usually begin with God's warning or condemnation, then move on to a picture of the Lord's plan for them in Messiah's future kingdom. In Isaiah 18, God is addressing the people who are 'beyond the rivers of Ethiopia.'"

He glanced up from his notes, then continued: "Moreover, Isaiah speaks prophetically of a procession traveling to Israel following the Second Coming, when Messiah returns triumphantly to establish His kingdom on earth."

My ears perked up. "Go on," I said.

HIS GLORIOUS RESTING PLACE

Ken led me through a number of prophetic Scriptures in which Jesus Himself promises He will return to a future, believing remnant of Israel to establish His righteous kingdom *over* Israel, *through* Israel, and over the whole earth. One of these verses, Matthew 19:28, states: *"So Jesus said to them, 'Assuredly I say to you, that in the regeneration, when the Son of Man sits on the throne of His glory, you who have followed Me will also sit on twelve thrones, judging the twelve tribes of Israel.'"*

Many other prophetic passages describe this glorious event (such as Daniel 7:13–14; Malachi 3:1; Micah 5:2; Isaiah 24:23). Yet, tucked within the lines of Isaiah 18 lay several references to the same event: Messiah's ultimate conquest and return to rule and reign as God and King in Jerusalem.

Ken continued, "It's a series of events called the Day of the Lord."

He read Isaiah 18:3, which states, *"When He lifts up a banner on the mountains..."* Then he carefully explained how its imagery could easily be linked to a Messianic prophecy in Isaiah 11: *"In that day the Root of Jesse will stand as a banner for the peoples; the nations will rally to him, and his resting place will be glorious"* (v.10 NIV). And again, reading from Isaiah 18:3: *"When he blows a trumpet, you hear it..."*

Ken flashed ahead to Messiah's return as prophesied in Zechariah: *"The Lord God will blow the trumpet"* (Zechariah 9:14). Then back to Isaiah 18:4 and the phrase, *"I will take My rest."*

He noted, "This parallels closely the phrase, *'And His resting place shall be glorious'* in Isaiah 11:10 and other passages."

Ken placed his notes on my desk and traced a finger down the page as if reviewing a checklist. "Bob, Isaiah 18 clearly refers to the Day of the Lord. I've checked it out thoroughly, and it's obviously talking prophetically about Messiah's return and conquest." He pulled another set of notes from a binder and said, "Now look at this."

He opened to a passage from the Book of Ezekiel, in which the prophet, in an angelic vision, saw and recorded the precise measurements, features, and configuration of the Messianic temple. Ezekiel's vision, almost neurotic in its detail, itemizes a painstaking sequence of events immediately following Christ's return.

According to Ezekiel 43, Christ will rule from a Messianic temple in Jerusalem and take His place on a throne:

> *"And the glory of the Lord came into the temple by way of the gate which faces toward the east. The Spirit lifted me up and brought me into the inner court; and behold, the glory of the Lord filled the temple. Then I heard Him speaking to me from the temple....And He said to me, 'Son of man, this is the place of My throne and the place of the soles of My feet, where I will dwell in the midst of the children of Israel forever'"* (Ezekiel 43:4–7).

It seemed plain enough: on that day, the Lord would come into His temple and dwell forever with His people, Israel. Yet, in an interesting twist, it also appears that Christ's own throne— *"the place of the soles of My feet"*—would reside within the Messianic temple. Never before in the Bible had another Hebrew king—David, Solomon, Josiah—ruled on a throne from inside the holy temple; always they executed their royal duties from within the palace.

BROUGHT FROM WHERE?

Mulling over these hopeful verses anticipating Christ's triumphant reappearance and His entrance into His temple and sitting on His throne, I momentarily forgot what any of it might have to do with Isaiah 18.

"Where are you going with this, Ken?" I asked.

"Watch this," he said. Then he flipped back to Isaiah: *"At that time gifts will be brought to the Lord Almighty from a people tall and smooth-skinned...to Mount Zion, the place of the Name of the Lord Almighty"* (Isaiah 18:7 NIV).

He closed the Book and concluded, "This verse categorically states that, at the time of Christ's glorious return to His Messianic temple, gifts will be brought to Mount Zion from Ethiopia—in the Name of the Lord Almighty." Years later, of course, I would come to believe this Zion was the placement of the real temples.

Ken looked at me and asked, "What do you think he means by *'the place of the Name of the Lord Almighty?'"*

I shrugged. "I could take a guess, but why don't you make it easier, and just tell me?"

Ken then began describing how, during his study of the Hebrew text of Isaiah 18 and a number of cross references, he thought he had noticed a pattern, something laced through Scripture that had never crossed his mind. Where exactly was "the place of the Name of the Lord Almighty"?

"If what I'm seeing is true," he observed, "we may well be framing the larger purpose and whereabouts of the Ark of the Covenant in these latter days in an entirely new context."

I listened, deeply engrossed, as Ken walked me through passage after passage confirming that the place of the "Name of the Lord" had, in Scripture, always been intimately associated with the holy temple. Moreover, by tracing this phrase from Deuteronomy to Jeremiah, this spot where the Lord's name could forever be found just happened to occupy the space directly above the Ark of the Covenant, within the Holy of Holies.

"What?" I asked, instantly aware that such a place also described the area between the wings of the cherubim on the mercy seat.

Ken turned back to the Old Testament and explained how the dwelling place of God's name was progressively revealed over time, from a broader meaning to a more specific usage, as God narrowed and further specified His revelation to Israel.

In Deuteronomy, for instance, the writer begins by identifying the place of God's name in the broadest possible terms, calling it *"the land"* He promised to His people (Deuteronomy 12:10-11).

In Jeremiah, God recalls the past and orders, *"But go now to My place which was in Shiloh, where I set My name at the first..."* (Jeremiah 7:12). Here, God referred to where the ark originally had been kept—that is, within the tabernacle at Shiloh (Joshua 18:1).

Finally, we follow this path forward to 1 Chronicles 13:6, where we are told: *"David and all Israel went up to Baalah, to Kirjath Jearim, which belonged to Judah, to bring up from there the ark of God the Lord, who dwells between the cherubim, where His name is proclaimed."*

In Ken's estimation, this final verse conclusively established the "place of His name" as residing above the Ark of the Covenant, stationed between the cherubim in the Holy of Holies.

ARRIVAL OF THE GIFT

Suddenly the conversation became much more interesting. As we continued to track the "place of My name" terminology throughout the Old Testament, the passages consistently referred not only to the holy temple but also to the Holy of Holies within the temple.

There could be no mistaking it: God's name would dwell in the temple forever: *"And the Lord said to him: 'I have heard your prayer and your supplication that you have made before Me; I have consecrated this house which you have built to put My name there forever, and My eyes and My heart will be there perpetually'"* (1 Kings 9:3).

More than that, it would reside forever in the Holy of Holies within the temple. Only one other item had ever been permitted within the Holy of Holies: the Ark of the Covenant.

Ken wore a cautious expression as, once again, he turned back to Isaiah 18:7—and gifts will be brought to *"the place of the Name of the Lord Almighty."*

"Without question, Bob," he exclaimed, "This verse is talking prophetically about gifts from Ethiopia being brought to the most holy place of a future temple." He paused, wary of my response. "Can you see it, Bob? We're talking about gifts arriving directly into the Holy of Holies of the temple, where the ark once resided...on the Day of the Lord."

I could see where Ken intended to go with this, though I had no intention of letting myself get carried away. "Okay Ken," I asked, "What kind of gifts?"

Ken answered, "Well, I checked the Hebrew on this word in verse 7, and strangely enough, in this passage the word *gifts* actually translates to 'gift.' It's singular, Bob. If I'm reading this right, one—and only one—important present will be brought out of Ethiopia at the return of Christ."

At that, we both fell silent. I imagined bold, colorful images of Axum monks marching in procession to Jerusalem with some ultimate, incomparable gift or offering. I had never heard or read of such an event in all my travels or research. Anticipating my thoughts, Ken broke our silence: "Isaiah seems to be telling us that a significant, singular gift will be brought in a procession to Israel from Ethiopia when the Lord returns to His Messianic temple."

He paused, then added, "According to Isaiah 18:7, biblical prophecy tells us this gift will be carried to the place of the *'name of the Lord of hosts,'* to *'Mount Zion,'* which must refer to the most holy place in the Messianic temple."

Spellbound, I barely heard Ken's next question, which he asked as slowly and deliberately as he could.

"Bob," he said quietly, "what is the only gift that could be worthy of being placed in the Holy of Holies of the Messianic temple?"

"The Ark of the Covenant," I exhaled, feeling the full force to my soul as I said it.

During the following weeks, the more we tried to discount the ark in Ethiopia theory, the more evidence we unearthed for something significant arriving from Ethiopia to occupy the most holy place in the Messianic temple. The ark just may have a profound obligation to future events and we were becoming more convinced with every new discovery in Scripture.

In the book of Zephaniah, it states, *"From beyond the rivers of Ethiopia my worshipers, the daughter of My dispersed ones, shall bring My offering"* (Zephaniah 3:10).

The offering described by Zephaniah is also singular. God's worshipers will bring Him a *gift.* Even more intriguing than the imagery of the gift is the Hebrew meaning of the word "bring." The term in Zephaniah 3:10 does not indicate a typical offering. The word, *yabal*—cited both in Isaiah 18 and Zephaniah 3—differs vastly from the common term, *bo,* in that it implies a bringing or leading forth *in an official or royal procession* (Job 10:19; 21:30; Psalm 45:14-15; 68:29; Isaiah 18:7)—a procession from Cush carrying an item of great importance to Jerusalem, from beyond the rivers of Ethiopia. Could it possibly be the Ark of the Covenant?

This gift would be brought all the way into the very place where His Name dwells forever—into the Holy of Holies of the Jerusalem temple. What could be worthy of being carried such a great distance, to the inside of the temple to Messiah—especially since traditional offerings are always received *outside* the temple?

What, indeed, other than the Ark of the Covenant.

THE THRONE

My days and nights seemed to blend together. I was excited and apprehensive at the same time. I was now intruding on the misty realm of future events described in Scripture, treading on the unfamiliar ground of Bible prophecy. For me, it was unsure footing. Yet, I was drawn by the possibilities. I decided to use God's Word as I always had, like a police investigator, and let the words of Scripture guide me through the smoky chambers of the prophets.

From the glow of my computer screen unfolded a much deeper mystery than I could have imagined. I saw the panorama of a golden ark being carried on poles by Hebrew priests from the Levitical Jews who now live on the shore of Lake T'ana. They would bring it as a gift to the temple in Jerusalem, and according to Ezekiel, this is the place of Christ's throne. *"Son of man, this is the place of My throne and the place of the soles of My feet, where I will dwell in the midst of the children of Israel forever"* (Ezekiel 43:7).

Ezekiel's words spoke of Christ's throne in the temple, the same temple that the gift from Ethiopia will occupy. These throne metaphors kept appearing, except they seemed to be more than metaphors. They looked suspiciously like future facts.

Zechariah, for example, provides a stirring account of the returning king as He reigns from His throne in the temple: *"From His place He shall branch out, and He shall build the temple of the Lord; yes, He shall build the temple of the Lord. He shall bear the glory, and shall sit and rule on His throne; So He shall be a priest on His throne, and the counsel of peace shall be between them both"* (Zechariah 6:12-13).

Verses like these, and many others, seem to portray the mercy seat of the ark as a throne. I began directing my gaze toward scriptural references to God's "throne," and started considering the mercy seat as something separate and distinct from the Ark of the Covenant. During Israel's wandering in the wilderness, the mercy seat (as God's throne) shone through from the ark's earliest appearance.

The image lingers of God speaking to Moses in the tabernacle: *"Now when Moses went into the tabernacle of meeting to speak with Him, he heard the voice of One speaking to him from above the mercy seat that was on the ark of the Testimony, from between the two cherubim; thus He spoke to him"* (Numbers 7:89).

Sometime later, when God had established the Hebrews in the land of Israel, David moved the tabernacle to the City of David, where the ark and mercy seat ultimately became the focus of Solomon's temple. King Solomon recounted this in 1 Kings, memorializing his father David's plans to build a temple for the Lord, saying, *"...And there I have made a place for the ark, in which is the covenant of the Lord which He made with our fathers, when He brought them out of the land of Egypt"* (1 Kings 8:21).

Solomon then called for the installation of the ark as God's throne in the newly constructed temple, praying, *"Now therefore, arise O Lord God, to Your resting place, You and the ark of Your strength"* (2 Chronicles 6:41).

Following Solomon's prayer, God consumed the sacrifices that had been offered, and *"the glory of the Lord filled the temple. And the priests could not enter the house of the Lord, because the glory of the Lord had filled the Lord's house"* (2 Chronicles 7:1-2).

Centuries later, Jesus would use the same imagery when He spoke prophetically of the Son of Man (Jesus Himself) coming *"in His glory, and all the holy angels with Him,"* adding, *"then He will sit on the throne of His glory"* (Matthew 25:31).

As incredible as it sounded, the biblical evidence kept mounting to commend the mercy seat of the ark as the literal, physical *throne* of the expected Messiah.

MOSAIC ON THE FLOOR

I started to see these Bible verses as a vast mosaic of tiny colored pieces of glass spread out on the floor; each verse made clearer the unfolding image. I began to input what I saw as cryptic messages from the prophets into my computer. For instance, in the wilderness wanderings, when the priests moved the ark, Moses said: *"Rise up O Lord! Let Your enemies be scattered, and let those who hate You flee before You"* (Numbers 10:35).

The almost identical words are found in Psalm 68:1: *"Let God arise, let His enemies be scattered; let those also who hate Him flee before Him."*

The following verses from this same psalm seized my attention and seemed as if they were a hidden message:

- *"They have seen Your procession, O God, the procession of my God, my King, into the sanctuary"* (verse 24).
- *"Because of your temple at Jerusalem, Kings will bring presents to You"* (verse 29).
- *"Ethiopia will quickly stretch out her hands to God"* (verse 31).

I knew we were standing on a radical new theory and that, for many traditionalists, it would not settle well. Bible passages kept mounting. However, the verse that set my heart racing came from the New Testament.

In the book of Acts, Luke records a significant encounter with a eunuch from Ethiopia. The event occurs shortly after Christ's death and resurrection. Luke, the writer of Acts, identifies the Ethiopian as a prominent official in the court of Candace, "Queen of the Ethiopians." The man managed her royal treasury and was on a visit to Jerusalem. Then the eunuch began his journey home. This is when Philip, guided by the Holy Spirit, ran up to the chariot and overheard the eunuch reading from Isaiah 53. The passage, Isaiah 53:7-8, foretold the crucifixion of Christ.

Most Christians know the rest of the story: Philip asked the eunuch if he understood what he was reading, and, informed of the man's befuddlement, Philip told the Ethiopian the good news of Christ. The encounter ended with the eunuch professing faith in the Savior and being baptized by Philip.

The account gives us a wonderful glimpse at a telling moment in the expansion of the church into northern Africa. But here we have to ask, "Is there more to Luke's story?"

What if we dared view the entire episode in a slightly different light—say, from the context of Isaiah 18—recalling that, centuries earlier, Isaiah foresaw some great offering coming forth from Ethiopia at the Messiah's triumphant return? By adjusting the slide under this microscope, we might see an otherwise minor passage move into sharp focus. Seen through the lens of Isaiah 18, Philip's encounter on the desert road may have extreme significance.

WHY DID HE COME?

We know that the eunuch had charge of all of Candace's treasures (Acts 8:27). But why, other than to worship, had this particular Ethiopian traveled to Jerusalem? And why had Luke bothered to record it? Why did Candace send a eunuch, and why did he carry in his chariot a cumbersome scroll of a prophet? Finally, why did Philip appear beside the chariot as the eunuch read from Isaiah 53? Could this episode shed light on the question of whether the ark and mercy seat lay in Ethiopia at that time?

The answers we propose might come as a shock and is triggered by the following verses: *"The Lord has made bare His holy arm in the eyes of all the nations; and all the ends of the earth shall see the salvation of our God. Depart! Depart! Go out from there, touch no unclean thing; go out from the midst of her, be clean, you who bear the vessels of the Lord"* (Isaiah 52:10-11).

The phrase, *"Go out from there...you who bear the vessels of the Lord"* seemed to shine like a neon light. It immediately precedes Isaiah 53, which prophesies Christ's suffering and death. No doubt the Ethiopian viewed Isaiah 52 and 53 as they should be—as two parts of a whole. Could he have received them as marching orders to make haste to Jerusalem to behold Messiah and bring Him the gift foretold by Isaiah, the Ark of the Covenant?

Could the Holy Spirit's insistence that Philip approach the eunuch be because the ark and mercy seat indeed lay hidden in northern Ethiopia? If the ark were there it would likely have been registered among Candace's royal treasury. And if the monarch of Ethiopia considered those vessels a holy trust to be held and protected until the arrival of Israel's Messiah, then the eunuch's purpose in visiting Jerusalem may well have been to determine whether the King's throne (the mercy seat) would now be required.

Could the royal emissary of those *"who bear the vessels of the Lord"* (Isaiah 52:10-11) actually be responding to Isaiah's prophesy alerting a great gift to be brought to Christ, to the temple in the stronghold of Zion, in the City of David, at the Gihon Spring?

DON'T OVERLOOK THE NEXT VERSE

In proposing a new theory, you always need to address troublesome verses that may waylay the premise. Jeremiah 3:16 seems to mangle the whole throne assumption. It reads, *"'In those days, when your numbers have increased greatly in the land,' declares the Lord, 'men will no longer say, "The Ark of the Covenant of the Lord." It will never enter their minds or be remembered; it will not be made anymore"* (NIV).

It seems from Jeremiah that in the future no one will care about the Ark of the Covenant. It will not spring to mind, nor will they remember it, nor will they visit it, nor will it be made anymore. But the very next verse makes a huge difference. The Ark of the Covenant, the wooden box that held the law, will no longer be the focus and, if our theory is correct, the pure gold top called the mercy seat will be used as a throne in the temple of the Lord. *"At that time Jerusalem shall be called The Throne of the Lord, and all the nations shall be gathered to it, to the name of the Lord, to Jerusalem"* (verse 17).

The ark will be no more; it is made of wood and wood decays. It is temporal and of no importance in the future. The wooden box has fulfilled its assignment in history. It held the stone tablets of the Law, but the blood offering that was placed on the mercy seat as a sin offering in the Old Testament is exactly where the sin offering of Christ will rest in the future temple. Christ will rule from this gold-lid throne in Jerusalem and all nations will gather in worship.

After all, what other object in all of the outstretched arms of infinity could be worthy of being the throne of our Lord except the pure gold mercy seat?

Chapter 18

A Final Word

If, at this point, I have not convinced the reader regarding any of this, that was not my intent. I simply wanted to open a sincere debate on the subjects we've been discussing.

I hope, at the very least, that seekers of truth will welcome dialog as to the location of the forgotten temples of God, the fate of the Ark of the Covenant, and the site of the future temples. The bottom line is this: truth will ultimately be sifted through the screen of Scripture and time—and what remains will be that of legitimacy.

Now, as the closing words in this book, I would like to offer my opinion as to what will happen in the meantime if the new temple location is not accepted as the true temple site.

I have been exploring, doing research and working with Muslim governments over twenty-eight years. I've lived with Muslims, had meals with them, and became friends with many. Once they even saved my life in Afghanistan.

In dimly lit rooms of their homes, most share the same concerns as the majority of Jews and Christians. They love their children and want them to have a good, peaceful, long life. I can even say that I have been treated by Muslim families in an extraordinarily hospitable and kind way. But there are Muslim extremists who contrast harshly with the peaceful factions. They simply hate Jews—all Jews—and want them dead.

I experienced this hatred of Jews first hand in 1988 when I was in Saudi Arabia doing research of the location of Mount Sinai. I, and my expedition partner, Larry Williams, were driving in the remote desert trying to find a lone vein of asphalt that bisected the

Saudi frontier. The road would take us to the town of Tabuk and from their, our flight home. Before we found our way out of that inhospitable wasteland, we were stopped by the Desert Frontier Forces and suspected of being some sort of spies. In short order, we were taken to an outpost of wool Bedouin tents with three mud hovels plugged into the side of the chalky cliffs. Two large, rusted tanks, supported by an off-kilter wooden platform, were the only landmarks. Some words were painted in block print on one of the weathered wood planks, but sandblasting windstorms had long since rendered the lettering illegible.

A gust of howling hot wind greeted me as I stepped from the truck, sweeping a spray of sand in my face and pelting my sunglasses with grit. Staring at me from the meager shade of the two tanks, a group of squatting Bedouin men sat wrapped in filthy, drab robes.

The whole village had an otherworldly, monochromatic look about it, as if it was dying and left to the fate of a pitiless desert. It apparently was the place where people came from miles around to fill their tanks with gas, get some water, and conduct their desert trade.

Six men in robes and brandishing old, battered rifles of the frontier forces, escorted us both to a mud-walled structure with patches of whitewash peeling from crumbling daub walls. A rifle butt prodded us along until we stood before a darkened doorway. I instinctively stopped short, but a foot against my lower back propelled me inside. Turning in anger, I could only make out the shape of a man standing in the entryway, his robed frame eclipsing the blinding rays of a harsh sun. As my eyes adjusted to the darkness, I heard the word *Jew* and felt warm spit trickle down my cheek.

Larry and I were pushed to the ground inside the hut and waited for the worst. Soon, a stocky man with a body built like an engine block and dressed in frayed military fatigues, barged his way past the other guards and tossed a camel's saddle on the floor. Dirt rose in the stifling air of the dimly lit room as the man made an exaggerated huff, and then lowered himself onto the saddle. He cocked his head and said nothing as if he wanted to read my mind. He had a brutish, sun-scarred face like blistered leather.

Larry and I sat on hard-packed sand, our backs now pressed against a wall stained dark with sweat and gun grease. They had confiscated our socks, shoes, keys, wallets, passports, and other papers, and had piled them in the middle of the room. Overhead, the rusted tin roof radiated triple-digit heat, and pencil-wide beams of sunlight pierced through holes in the roof, further searing my already burnt skin. I felt like a hapless ant at the mercy of a half-dozen school boys with magnifying glasses in their hands and a mean streak in their souls. I lowered my head and waited for the questioning to begin—fuming words shouted in a language I didn't understand. My answers—and Larry's—were equally incomprehensible to our captors.

Our Bedouin guards started in on us again and again, grilling us incessantly with unintelligible, mind-numbing questions. Even though no one understood a thing we said, they kept the questions heaping with anger-laced tirades and gun barrels swinging. One word that I did understand chilled my blood. The men kept calling us "Jews!"—and I had never before seen such vehement hatred.

How we got free from our captors is a pretty amazing story itself, and better relayed at another time, but for me the illustrated point is that I have seen and experienced first-hand the hatred of certain Muslim radicals.

THE FINAL SOLUTION

Years later, I found myself in Jerusalem when Muslims flowed into the city headed directly for the Al Haram Al-Sharif, aka Temple Mount. I could see the same look of animosity in most of their eyes that I remember so vividly while under arrest in that far away Arabian cell. The truth of the matter is this: nothing will change their minds and hearts in their deep enmity against the Jews. The hatred is woven in their genes, the detest is reinforced by their familial loyalties, radical teachings and violent actions of those around them. Allah will praise them if they should kill or be killed fighting the infidels. And the feud continues.

But the Bible speaks of a time when God's Son will return to earth and all knees shall bow and every tongue will confess that Jesus Christ is Lord. Christ's return is, and shall be, the final and only solution to hate and suffering. He is the Way, the Truth, and the Life, and no man can come to the Father but by Him (John 14:6).

In the meantime, and in the foreseeable future, the antichrist will enter the prophetic landscape. The appearance of a false peace will accompany him. It will all be a lie and short-lived, because in a heinous way the antichrist will defile the *Tribulation* temple, ushering a holocaust. However, he will be defeated by Christ and the new *Millennial* temple will rise from the ruins of the same place where both Solomon and Herod built temples.

All true temples of God will then have been laminated in proper layers one over another in the precincts of the original stronghold of Zion and in the ancient City of David. This will happen in God's timing, for His purpose, for His glory and nothing will in any way modify the inevitability of that divine plan.

TEMPLES EVERYWHERE

In presenting this book, I wondered how it would be received by the clergy. Most all pastors, it seems, have taken tours to the Temple Mount in Jerusalem and were pointed to the high stone walls and told with confident surety that this was indeed the location of Solomon's temple. The people that they led snapped photos, believing that they had a camera full of images that captured a revered biblical landmark.

I sent the manuscript to several pastors for comment and suggestions, and was most pleased at the unexpected favorable, and at times, exuberant responses. However the reaction from one particular minister, John Knapp of Green Valley Calvary

Chapel in Nevada, worried me. He shepherds a fairly large church, running four services, but the one thing that makes him different than most is that his church has pictures of the Temple Mount and other such images of the temple all over the facility. He has temple paintings in the foyer, displayed down the halls, and in his office. Just two days before I handed in this manuscript to the editor I was a guest speaker at his church, and after seeing all his temple memorabilia and paintings from Israel, I affectionately called Pastor John the *"temple man."*

I wondered how he, of all people, would react to the theory of the temple not being on the Temple Mount. This man had preached to his congregation about the temple in Jerusalem, taken tours there, prayed at the site, and believed whole-heartedly that the former temple of Solomon was indeed unequivocally without any question located on the traditional Temple Mount platform.

At dinner that night at Pastor John's home along with his wife, Amber, and three sons sitting at their dining table, I explained my temple theory with the aid of a handful of notes. It was not easy, his sons had a Temple Mount model that they excitedly showed me as I was reading from some of my supporting Bible verses.

When I was finished, the pastor just stared at me. It was an awkward moment of stone silence, no questions were forthcoming, not even a slight indication as to what he was thinking. His eyes then scanned the faces of his children and his wife as he said slow and sure, "I am dogmatic in all my beliefs, but correcting truth, no matter when or where it comes from, is always stronger that my own opinions."

Pastor John raked his silver-streaked hair back, "I really can't find one thing that would give me reason that you are not absolutely right."

I hardly knew what to say. Here was a man of deep conviction who was willing to look past a tradition that was exorbitantly well entrenched in his faith structure. Yet he was intellectually honest enough that he was obliged to shift those deep-rooted paradigms of belief based on revealing biblical text.

For me, I think that the Temple Mount has been unchallenged

for so long now as to its validity of placement that we somehow, someway, simply forgot the correct assignment of God's holy mountain.

I hope and pray that whether scholar, student, pastor, or neophyte, we let God's Word be the ultimate mediator and final arbitrator on the temple, the ark, and beyond.

But you are those who forsake
the Lord, who forget My holy mountain.
– Isaiah 65:11

FOOTNOTES

Chapter 2

1. Surah 8:39.
2. Carlson, Ron, and Decker, Ed., *Facts on False Teachings,* Harvest House, 2003, p.110.
3. Armstrong, Karen, *Holy War: The Crusades and Their Impact on Today's World,* Anchor Books, 2001, p.1.
4. Armstrong, p.179.
5. Armstrong, p.452.
6. Hunt, David, *A Woman Rides the Beast,* Harvest House Publications, 1994, p.268.
7. Hunt, p.23.
8. Collins, Larry, and LaPierre, Dominique, *O Jerusalem,* Simon & Schuster, 1972.

Chapter 3

1. Michell, John, *The Temple At Jerusalem,* Samuel Weiser, Inc., 1990, p.12). Former Palestinian Authority official Nabil Sha'ath called the temple "fictitious" and Palestinian academic Hamed Salem referred to the temples as "fiction" and "fantasy" (Shanks, Hershel, *in Jerusalem's Temple Mount,* Biblical Archaeology Society, 2007, pp.4-5).
2. Michell, pp.25-26.
3. Michell, p.2.
4. Shanks, Hershel, in *Jerusalem's Temple Mount,* Biblical Archaeology Society, 2007.
5. Rosen-Ayalon, Myriam, *The Early Islamic Monuments of Al-Haram Al-Sharif,* Hebrew University of Jerusalem, 1988, p.7.
6. Solomon, Gershon, quoted in Price, Randal, *The Temple and Bible Prophecy,* Harvest House, 2005, p.174.
7. Montefiore, Simon Sebag, *Monsters: History's Most Evil Men and Women,* Quercus Publishing, 2009, p.27.

Chapter 4

1. Martin, Edward, *The Temples That Jerusalem Forgot,* Academy for Scriptural Knowledge, 1994, pp.60,66.
2. Vos, Howard F., *Nelson's New Illustrated Bible Manners and Customs,* Thomas Nelson, Inc., 1999, p.406.

3. Josephus, *Jewish Wars,* V5.8.
4. Dando-Collins, Stephen, *Legions of Rome, the Definitive History of Every Imperial Roman Legion,* St. Martin's Press, 2010, p.354.
5. Dando-Collins, p.316.
6. Grant, Michael, *The Twelve Caesars,* Barnes & Noble, 1996, p.228.

Chapter 5

1. Josephus, *Jewish Wars,* V. 2, I.I.
2. Dando-Collins, p.66.
3. Wilkinson, John, *Egeria's Travels,* Aris & Phillips, 1999, p.22.
4. Martin, pp.79-81.
5. Martin, p.97.
6. Tactius, *The Histories,* Penguin, 2009, p.306.
7. Shanks, Herhel, editor, "Excavating in the Shadow of the Temple Mount," *Bible Archaeological Review,* Nov., 1986, pp.20,32.
8. Shanks, Hershel, *Jerusalem's Temple Mount,* Biblical Archaeology Society, 2007, p.58.
9. Mare, W. Harold, *The Archaeology of the Jerusalem Area,* Wiph & Stock Publishers, 2002, p.193.
10. Shanks, p.40.
11. Josephus, V.2, pp.395-406.
12. Martin, p.29.
13. Josephus, V.5, p.8.
14. Martin, p.429.
15. Goodman, Martin, *Rome and Jerusalem: The Clash of Ancient Civilizations,* Vintage Books, 2007, p.422.

Chapter 6

1. Horovitz, Ahron, *City of David: The Story of Ancient Jerusalem,* Lamda Publishers, 2009, p. 67.
2. Mare, W. Harold, *The Archaeology of the Jerusalem Area,* Wiph & Stock Publishers, 2002, p.99.
3. Benjamin, Sarah, *The World of Benjamin Tudela,* Farleigh Dickinson University Press, 1995, p.171.
4. Eusebius, *The Proof of the Gospel,* Book VIII, Chapter 3, section 405, 406. Edited and translated by W. J. Ferrar in 1920 and reprinted by Baker Book House, 1981.

5. Josephus, *Contra Apion,* 1:22.

Chapter 7

1. Horovitz, p.106.

Chapter 8

1. Hammer, Reuven, *The Jerusalem Anthology,* The Jewish Publication Society, 1995, p.148.
2. Josephus, *Jewish Wars,* V.8.
3. Martin, pp.288, 289.
4. Shutt, R.J.H., translation in James A. Charlesworth's *The Old Testament Pseudepigrapha Vol. II,* Doubleday, 1985, p.18.
5. Tacitus, Book 5, para.12.
6. Maier, Johann, *The Temple Scroll,* Col. XXXII, 12-13 (F.G. Martinez translation).
7. Vilnay, Zev, *Legends of Jerusalem,* Jewish Publication Society, 1973 edition. (Account of Eliyahu ha-Cohen, Midrash Talpioth, and Emerek ha-Melech).
8. *Gemara, Babylonian Talmud.* Tractate Tamid 31b, Soncino Press, 1961 edition, pp. 25-26.

Chapter 9

1. Mare, p.203.
2. Shanks, p.52

Chapter 10

1. Maier, Johann, *The Temple Scroll,* Col. XXXII, 12-13 (F. G. Martinez translation).

Chapter 11

1. Shanks, p.33.
2. Sakurai, Gail, *The Jamestown Colony,* Grolier Publishing, 1997, p. 26.
3. *The Epistle of Barnabas,* 16:16.
4. Josephus, *Antiquities,* XV, 11, 3.
5. Sagiv, Tuvia, *The Hidden Secrets of the Temple Mount,* 1996, www.templemount.org/tempmt.html
6. Shanks, p.69.
7. Eusebius, *Ecclesiastical History,* IX, x, 7-11, Hendrickson Publishers, 1998 edition.

Chapter 13

1. Horovitz, p.280.
2. Horovitz, p.280.
3. Horovitz, p.280.
4. Shanks, p. 119.
5. Josephus, *Jewish Wars,* V.5,8.
6. Levine, Lee, *Union Reform Judiasm Magazine,* Winter, 2007.

Chapter 14

1. Price, Randall , *The Temple and Bible Prophecy,* Harvest House, 2005, p. 531.

Chapter 15

1. Silberman, Neil Asher, *Digging for God and Country: Exploration, Archaeology and the Secret Struggle for the Holy Land, 1799-1917,* Knofp, Inc., 1982, pp. 88-99.

Chapter 16

1. Porten, Bezaleel, *Archives From Elephantine: The Life of an Ancient Jewish Military Colony,* University of California Press, 1968, pp.109,152.
2. Cornfeld, Gaalya, *Archaeology of the Bible Book by Book,* Harper and Row, 1976, pp.25, 118.
3. Hancock, Graham Hancock, *The Sign and the Seal,* Touchstone, 1993, p. 216.

Chapter 17

1. Blaiklock, E.M. and Harrison, R.K., editors, *New International Dictionary of Biblical Archaeology,* Zondervan Publishing House, 1983, p.177.

Acknowledgments

No book of this nature could ever be possible without many people offering their generous help and intellect. I would like to first thank my lovely wife Terry and my twins Shannon and Connor who daily inspired me during this literary process. Then there is researcher Bonnie Dawson who made this all possible with her enormous helping heart and always encouraging spirit.

Nora Christensen, Ray Ardizzone, Carole Ardizzone, Pete Leininger and Barbara Leininger gave me an incredible helping hand when it was the most needed. Ernest Martin, Graham Hancock and Ken Durham provided much intellectual resource material that lifted this work beyond what I ever could have done without their amazing insights.

Many others helped generously as well, such as Barbara Anne Klein, David Weisman, John Nill, Rhonda Sand, Frank Turek, Paul Feinberg, Mike Barnes, Eli Shukron, Dan Hayden, Craig and Meredith Newmaker, Norm Andersson, Chuck Benson, Mary Irwin, Tom and Kim Bengard, James Stock, Paul and Nancy Cornuke, Gary Smeltzer, Robbie Meadows, Bob Hey, Philip Thompson, Perry Sanders, Gary Harding, Don McDonald, Bobby Brown, Jay lee, Bill Zerella, Doug and Joan Wenzel, Boone Powell, Chuck Missler, David Halbrook, Sig Swanstrom, and my editor Neil Eskelin.

For Additional Resources
or to Schedule the Author for
Speaking Engagements, Contact:

Robert Cornuke
Bible Archaeological Search
and Exploration Institute (BASE)
P.O. Box 545
Monument, Colorado 80132

Phone: 719-488-4228
Email: Basebobc@aol.com
Internet: www.Baseinstitute.org